# The Art of Drinksmanship

Golden Hands Books

Marshall Cavendish
London and New York

All modern glassware from a large and splendid selection at Heals, Tottenham Ct. Rd. London W1—Dansk teak board on page 53 at Liberty, Regent St, London W1. Terrine of paté from Robert Carrier. Silver at Lewis & Kaye, 1B Albemarle St, London W1. Modern chess set at Aspreys, Bond St, London W1. Antique glass at Burne Ltd, 11 Elystan St, London SW3. Our thanks go to the following companies for their help in preparing this book—
John Harvey & Sons Ltd, for supplying the Sherries on page 13.
Allied Breweries, for supplying many of the drinks for the cocktails, liqueurs and wine photography.
The Vintage House, Old Compton St, London W1 for loaning all the bottles of aperitifs.

**Photo credits:**
Alan Duns—pp 6, 11, 13, 21, 27, 29, 31, 35, 37, 44, 47, 55, 61.
John Marmaras—p15.
Syndication International—pp 9, 49.
Harvey's Sherry—p13.
J. Allen Cash—p13.
Camera Press (Uggla) p15 (Kjell Nilsson) p17.
H. Von Sterneck pp 17, 40.
Michael Boys—pp 17, 42, 51, 59.
W & A Gilbey Ltd—p27.
Michael Leale—p27.
Christine Pearcy—p33.
Baehr Pictures—p60.
Nino Mascardi of Epipress—p23
Illustrations
Roy Flooks—p18.
Laurence Henry—p24.
Anna Barnard, Garden Studio—p62.

**Editor** — Karen Harriman

**Authors**
Spirits and Cocktails and a Matter of Proof —John Doxat, author of Drinks and Drinking published by Ward, Lock
Sherry and Madeira —Julian Jeffs, author of Sherry, published by Faber
Wine —John Marshall, wine correspondent of the Evening News

Parties, Punches and Summer Coolers —Margaret Sherman, hostess editor of Good Housekeeping, and Keith F. Bean, contributor to A Dictionary of Gastronomy published by the International Wine & Food Society

What to drink with what ... and a few suggestions —Penelope Berners Price (Penelope Maxwell of House & Garden's Wine & Food section)
Cognac & Port, and Choosing glasses —Ian Dunlop
Before a meal-aperitifs —Peter Jeeves, former publisher of Wine & Food
Beer and Stout —Duncan Gardiner
Dips and Dunks —Delia Smith

Published by
Marshall Cavendish Publications Limited,
58 Old Compton Street,
London W1V 5PA.

© Marshall Cavendish Limited 1972

This material was first published by Marshall Cavendish Limited in the special *All You Need to Know About Drinks*

This volume first published 1975

Printed in Great Britain by Ben Johnson & Co Ltd

ISBN 0 85685 093 4

This volume is not to be sold in the USA, Canada or the Philippines

# INTRODUCTION

Whether you're an experienced drinker or about to take your first taste of something alcoholic; a serious student of fine wine or a nervous buyer of Spanish plonk—this book is for you.

For the spirits drinker there's a concise but informative guide to the 'big five' (vodka, rum, gin, whisky and brandy) plus lots of interesting ideas for mixed drinks and cocktails—have you ever tasted Forbidden Fruit or Sloe Gin? For the would-be wine connoisseur, there's a no-nonsense survey of the world's major (and minor) wines, red, white, and rosé, together with some sensible tips on that thorny question of which wine to serve with which food (there's a tell-at-a-glance chart, too, for those who're still confused by that last erudite wine-and-food book they read!) And, in addition, there's lots of information on fortified wines (sherry, port and Madeira), liqueurs, and those marvellous old favourites beer and cider.

Party-givers aren't forgotten either—there are pages and pages of delicious punch recipes, guaranteed to make a party swing, plus some delectable dips to make sure their potency isn't too effective too quickly. (Don't despair if your taste runs to very lightly alcoholic or non-alcoholic drinks—they're well catered for, too). And, just in case your guests prefer coffee, there are some exciting tips for cheering it up with a shot of something fragrantly alcoholic!

It's compulsive reading—so whether you're planning a party, wondering what to drink with duck for dinner, or buying a drink in a bar, you'll find lots of ideas in this beautiful book.

# CONTENTS

# SPIRITS AND COCKTAILS

*There are a great many spirits in the world. But what we now normally call spirits embrace the five in widespread everyday use—Whisky, Gin, Vodka, Rum and Brandy. And for present purposes, we are applying the word 'cocktail' to some mixed drinks—long and short—associated with these principal spirits. They're well worth the flourish if you have time and panache.*

## SPIRITS

Spirits are produced by distillation: from a mildly alcoholic liquor, the alcohol is collected and concentrated. Alcohol vaporizes at 78·3°C and water at 100°C; theoretically you have only to bring the original brew to 78·3°C, to separate the alcohol from the water. Basic distillation can take place in the traditional pot-still, or in a more complicated patent-still, where distillation can be carried on continuously.

## COCKTAILS

When cocktails are not made in the glass from which they will be drunk, most cocktails can be, and many should be, mixed: drinks containing heavy cordials improve by being shaken in a cocktail-shaker (though it's not essential). Use ice generously in all cases, except where stated. In recipes, numbers refer to quantities of a measure, or fractions of it: a measure is a standard 1 fluid ounce (30-millilitre) jigger.

## WHISKY AND WHISKEY

### Whisky, Scotch

This is the world's most prestigious and internationally-enjoyed spirit. The art of distilling came to Scotland with Christian monks from Ireland at an early date. Whisky was known to the Scottish Royal Court in Edinburgh in 1500. It had a turbulent social history. It was a cottage industry: most crofters were distillers. Efforts to control and tax production, especially in the Highlands, were notably unsuccessful till the 1820s. Scotch Whisky was little appreciated in England, except in the extreme North, until the introduction in the 1860s of Blended Whisky, combining the robustness of Malt Whisky with the blandness of Grain Whisky. Rather less than a century ago, pioneer Scottish blenders started onslaughts on the English—and later the world—market which proved immensely successful. Malt Whisky is made by allowing barley briefly to sprout, the water used being of prime importance. The malted barley is dried by peat fires: this is vital. It is then coarsely ground. Hot water is added and from this mash a sweetish liquid (wort) is drawn. Yeast is added to the wort, which ferments, and this becomes the alcoholic wash (about 10% alcohol). The wash goes into a pot-still. The resultant spirit (low wines) is transferred into another and similar still, which produces Malt Whisky. It is matured in oak casks for a legal minimum of three years, but normally considerably longer.

Grain Whisky is produced by the patent-still process and is rarely matured beyond the legal minimum. It is used for marrying with Malt Whisky to produce the many brands of Blended Scotch Whisky which represent about 95% of all Scotch Whisky sold. Scotch Whisky averages about 50% each of Malt and Grain.

The number of individual Malts in a good blend can be as many as sixty: in the case of lesser brands it may only be a fraction of good Malt to give character and a very high percentage of Grain.

### Whiskey, Irish

This has greatly lost popularity in England, though it's enjoying a mild resurgence of interest through Irish Coffee. Whiskey was, in legend at least, distilled in Ireland 1,000 years ago. In Eire distilling is concentrated in the hands of an amalgamation of the three main distilleries. In Ulster there is only one distillery, the famous Bushmills. The mash for Irish Whiskey is barley (usually only half of it is malted), wheat, rye and—peculiar to Ireland—oats. Pot-stills are used, and three separate distillations. Irish Whiskey is distinctively more pungent than Blended Scotch. It has by law to be matured for seven years.

### Whiskey, American

The law specifies 30 types of American Whiskey, but only one name is protected by Act of Congress—Bourbon. This is the type mostly known overseas. Bourbon is made from a mash containing not less than 51% corn (maize). (Rye Whiskey has a mash of a minimum of 51% rye.) American Whiskey must be distilled at comparatively low strength and matured in new casks, which means that Bourbon is rather highly flavoured. After much agitation, a major US Whiskey company gained federal approval to distil an American 'Light' Whiskey at a higher strength and to mature it in previously used casks. This was only released from bond in July, 1972, so what commercial success this new type of Whiskey—4 years old—will finally enjoy remains to be seen.

### Whisky, Canadian

This is the fourth important regional Whisk(e)y. Canadian Whisky is made from a mash mostly of corn, with rye, wheat and some malted barley. Patent-rather than pot-still distillation is the rule, and the Whisky tends to be light in flavour; perhaps the best description of it is that it is half way between Scotch and the better American Rye Whiskies. It is widely distributed in Britain and even more so in the USA.

## COCKTAILS BASED ON VARIOUS TYPES OF WHISK(E)Y

**Atholl Brose**
1½ Scotch;
1 each pure cream and clear honey.
Mix in warm glass. Allow to cool.
Or omit cream and top with hot milk.

**Blood and Sand**
½ each Scotch, Cherry Brandy, fresh orange juice, Sweet Vermouth. Shake. Strain into adequate glass.

**Bobby Burns**
1½ Scotch; ¾ Sweet Vermouth; Teaspoon Benedictine. Stir. Strain into cocktail glass. Squeeze lemon rind over.

**Rob Roy**
½ each Scotch and Sweet Vermouth. Shake.

**Whisky Mac**
Equal proportions Scotch and Ginger Wine. No ice.

**Toddy**
Teaspoon sugar in warm glass, dissolved with little boiling water; 2 Scotch. Stir, top with boiling water and add more Scotch to taste.

**Rusty Nail**
Half-and-half Scotch and Drambuie, 'on the rocks' with twist of lemon.

**Highball**
2 Whisk(e)y (Bourbon or other) over ice in tall glass filled with soda.

**Manhattan**
1 Bourbon; ½ each Dry and Sweet Vermouth; dash Angostura Bitters. Stir. Strain into cocktail glass. Add cocktail cherry.

**Old Fashioned**
In small tumbler, teaspoon sugar; 3 dashes Angostura; 3 ice cubes; 2 Bourbon (or Canadian).

**Serpent's Tooth**
1 Irish; 2 Sweet Vermouth; 1 lemon juice; ½ Kummel, dash Angostura. Stir. Strain.

# GIN

For practical purposes this means the London Dry Gin type, made all over the world, but generally conceded to be at its finest when the production of a handful of London-based firms of some antiquity; the oldest dates from 1740. Dry Gin evolved from Unsweetened Gin, brought in about 100 years ago in contrast to sugary cordial 'Hollands' or 'Old Tom'. Gins vary greatly in taste—and often in quality.

There are many practical short cuts to making Gin. At its best it will be based on a pure neutral spirit. This spirit will be rectified (re-distilled) which further purifies it and this may be why that connoisseur of good living, the late André Simon, classified Gin as 'the purest of all spirits'. This rectified spirit is flavoured by various methods with salubrious juniper. This is essential to all true Gin: the name is a corruption of the old Dutch Genever (Geneva)—juniper. Oil of juniper has long been valued medicinally. Another ingredient is coriander, and there are further botanical ingredients in use; their numbers and proportions form the closely guarded formulae of the distillers. Gin is now in universal use, but only comparatively lately has it become respectable and a drink for women as well as men. In its earlier history Gin was associated with working-class drunkeness and, especially in London, was imbibed in vast quantities—often illicitly distilled. Perhaps the coming of the Cocktail Age (a spin-off from Prohibition in the USA) did as much as anything to make Gin fashionable as opposed to popular.

The other main Gin, once much drunk in England, is Dutch (Geneva) Gin. This is much more pungent than London Dry Gin and is for drinking

1    2    3    4    5

chilled and straight.
Plymouth Gin, a famous proprietary brand from that city, has a particular association with Pink Gin (Gin with a touch of Angostura).

## CLASSIC COCKTAILS BASED ON GIN

Most of the 'classic' cocktails that have stood the test of time were based on Dry Gin.

**Dry Martini**
2 Gin; ¼ Dry Vermouth (or less in modern use). Stir. Strain. Squeeze lemon rind over, not immersing. Olive optional.

**Bronx**
½ Gin; ¼ each Sweet and Dry Vermouth; juice of ¼ orange. Shake. Strain.

**Clover Club**
1 Gin; ½ Grenadine syrup; juice ½ lemon; white of 1 egg. Shake briskly. Strain.

**Gibson**
As Dry Martini but with a cocktail onion, instead of an olive.

**Gimlet**
Half-and-half Gin and lime juice cordial. Stirred, shaken, 'on the rocks' with or without splash soda.

**Gin Fizz**
1 Gin; juice ½ lemon; ½ tablespoon powdered sugar. Shake. Strain. Add soda.

**Gin Rickey**
2 Gin 'on the rocks'; ½ teaspoon Grenadine; juice ½ lemon which is then crushed into drink. (Rickeys may be made with other spirits).

**Gin Sling**
Juice 1 lemon; heaped teaspoon sugar; 2 Gin; dash Angostura; 'on the rocks' with a little water.

**Horse's Neck**
Hang spiral of lemon peel in tall glass; 2 Gin (or other spirit); top with Dry Ginger Ale.

**Negroni**
2 Gin; 1 each Sweet Vermouth and Campari 'on the rocks'; add soda, slice orange.

**Silver Streak**
1 Gin 'on the rocks'; ½ each lemon juice and Kummel.

**Singapore Gin Sling**
2 Gin; juice 1 lemon; heaped teaspoon sugar. Mix in tall glass; add soda, ½ each Cointreau and Cherry Brandy. Stir. Slice lemon. Straws.

**Collins**
As Gin Sling, but soda instead of water.

**White Lady**
½ Gin; ¼ each lemon juice and Cointreau; teaspoon egg white (optional). Shake. Strain.

**Trinity**
1 each Gin, Sweet Vermouth, Dry Vermouth. Mix. Strain.

## VODKA

This can mean two things. There are Russian or Polish Vodkas, of various types but usually delicately flavoured. These are best drunk very cold and neat as an accompaniment to tasty titbits. But for most people, Vodka means the Anglo-American spirit that is as lacking in taste as it is possible for a spirit to be. The term Anglo-American is used advisedly: the modern vogue for Vodka-drinking started in the USA and can actually be pin-pointed to the Cock 'n Bull Tavern, Los Angeles, where was invented the 'Moscow Mule' (Vodka, iced ginger beer and lime or lemon juice). The 'Moscow Mule' became fashionable on the trend-setting West Coast, and soon Vodka mixes spread across the country. It took a decade for Vodka to get anything like a similar hold in Britain, where Vodka is usually a pure spirit carefully filtered through a special form of charcoal. Its main merit is that it adds zest to whatever it is mixed with without giving any additional taste. By its purity it is held by some to be less productive of hang-overs than other spirits.
Vodka can be used for nearly all drinks traditionally based on Gin.

6       7       8       9       10

# A MATTER OF PROOF

Many countries are involved in the subject of Proof Spirit, both technically and in everyday explanation of the strength of alcoholic beverages—notably spirits. In part this is 'consumer protection'. However, its value in this direction is doubtful as only a handful of drinkers understand the Proof system.

There are three principal methods for indicating the strength of spirits, liqueurs, and sometimes of wines and aperitifs.

There is the British Proof system (sometimes called Sykes after the inventor of the hydrometer employed to test spirits); the US Proof; and the simple Metric (called Gay Lussac after its originator in France). British Proof is also used in Canada, Australia, New Zealand, the Commonwealth generally, and in Ireland and South Africa. Under the British Proof system absolute alcohol is 175.25 (in practice, 175) and Proof Spirit 100. This makes British Proof Spirit 57% alcohol: we use round figures for convenience.

The USA Proof system is different from the British. In the US Proof scale, absolute (pure) alcohol is rated at 200 and Proof Spirit as 100; ie 100 US Proof indicates a mixture of 50% alcohol and 50% water. US Proof terms can be translated into alcoholic strength simply by halving the Proof number: thus, 86 Proof (US) is 43% alcohol.

The Gay Lussac system applies in most other areas, and indicates the volume of pure alcohol in a beverage. (The Germans differ slightly, using weight instead of volume.)

Unfortunately, it is not simple to translate British Proof into American Proof or into Gay Lussac terms.

However, the normal strength of spirits in Britain is 70 Proof, which, conveniently, is 80 Proof (US) or 40 Gay Lussac; that is, contains 40% alcohol by volume.

There are many variations, due to national preferences, but the table below shows roughly the average strengths of spirits in some countries:

An important point to remember is, when examining the strength indicated on a bottle, to see in what system the strength is marked. Under both Proof systems—Gay Lussac is simplicity itself—it is essential to bear in mind that Proof Spirit is *not* pure spirit. Particularly in Britain, some wines fortified with spirit (latterly with Whisky) are labelled as '31% Proof Spirit'—thus not attracting full spirit tax: they contain about 17% alcohol.

The word Proof comes from the days when scientific precision in assessing the strength of spirits had not yet evolved. The method then was to add a mixture of water and spirit to gunpowder, the mixture being made progressively stronger until a point when the gunpowder would not be neutralized by the water but would burn explosively when fire was applied. Spirit which would cause this conflagration was said to have been 'proved'.

|  | Gin | Vodka | Whisky Rum Brandy |
|---|---|---|---|
| Britain (Sykes) | 70 | 65.5 | 70 |
| Canada (Sykes) | 75 | 70-80 | 70 |
| Australia (Sykes) | 75 | 70 | 75 |
| N.Zealand (Sykes) | 75 | 70 | 75 |
| S.Africa (Sykes) | 75 | 70-80 | 75 |
| USA (US Proof) | 86-94 | 80-100 | 86-100 |
| Europe, Latin America etc. (Gay Lussac) | 40-47 | 38-50 | 43 upwards |

A further simplified table may help illustrate the systems:

| British Proof (Sykes) | American (US Proof) | Gay Lussac (Metric) | Percentage of alcohol by volume |
|---|---|---|---|
| 175 | 200 | 100 | 100 |
| 100 | 114 | 57 | 57 |
| 88 | 100 | 50 | 50 |
| 80 | 90 | 45 | 45 |
| 75 | 86 | 43 | 43 |
| 70 | 80 | 40 | 40 |
| 65 | 74 | 37 | 37 |
| 0 | 0 | 0 | 0 |

*approximate comparisons*

# VODKA-BASED COCKTAILS

**Vodkatini**
As for Dry Martini but increase amount of Dry Vermouth and immerse lemon peel (or use grapefruit rind for a change).

**Bloody Mary**
Start with 2 Vodka 'on the rocks', add tomato juice; Tabasco; cayenne pepper; celery salt; Worcester Sauce—and anything else you care to. Stir.

**Bullshot**
Can of condensed consommé; 2 Vodka; celery salt, and continue as for Bloody Mary. Stir well. Strain.

**Bloody Bullshot**
Combination of two cocktails above.

**Screwdriver**
Equal amounts Vodka and iced orange juice.

**Harvey Wallbanger**
The above, plus Galliano liqueur.

**Black Russian**
Half-and-half Vodka and Kahlua liqueur 'on the rocks'.

# RUM

It is not known whence comes this rum word: it could be from 'rumbustious' (which once meant strong liquor), or from the Latin *saccahrum* (sugar), from a corruption of the Spanish *Ron* or the French *Rhum*, or even from the Devonian dialect 'Rumbullion'. Under English law, it is defined as a spirit distilled from sugar cane in sugar-producing countries. Rum is widely produced throughout the world, including the West Indies. In early times Rum was a crude spirit for fortifying slaves and it earned such nicknames as 'kill devil'. Not till the early 1700s did it gain any repute. Whilst some special Rums are produced in pot-stills, the main production is now by patent distillation on a very large scale. The alcoholic wash from which Rum is distilled is made by adding water to molasses, (by-product in the manufacture of cane sugar) which ferments rapidly. The spirit that comes from the stills is colourless and may be more or less highly flavoured, since patent distillation gives wide latitude of control in this matter. Heavy dark Rums—except for de luxe qualities produced by pot-stills—have added to them a concentrated, and highly refined and coloured, sugar distillate. Rum must be matured in wood for a minimum of three years for the British market.

Currently, light, white Rum is rapidly growing in popularity.

**Daiquiri**
1 White Rum; ½ each fresh lemon juice

*Cuba Libre – one of the simplest cocktails and great for summer time.*

(lime if available) and Grenadine. Shake. Strain. Serve very cold.

## Cuba Libre

White Rum 'on the rocks' in tall glass. Top with Cola (some fresh lemon juice optional).

# BRANDY

Brandy certainly derives from the Dutch *brandewijn* (burnt wine): 'burning' was once a word indicating distilling. The word covers a lot of spirits, from various bases. 'Grape Brandy' covers matured distillations of wine; it can come from many countries. But it is to France that we primarily look when thinking in terms of quality Brandy. Many experts rate Armagnac very highly: it is a single distillation and needs specially long

ageing in wood. Production is about a quarter that of Cognac and here we come to the Brandy that most people automatically think of when the word is used.

Cognac Brandy as we understand it came into being in the seventeenth century when second distillation (to capture the 'soul of the wine') started. For centuries the fresh white wines of the Charente area—once a proud possession of the English throne—had been exported. As early as the fifteenth century a primitive form of low-strength distilling was used to concentrate these wines and preserve them.

The white wine from which Cognac comes is not good wine: it is harsh and strong. But it makes the finest Brandy.

As soon as the wine is made in the autumn, distilling may commence. Pot-stills of no great size are used, the type being closely regulated. The first distillation produces the *brouilli* (rather under 30% alcohol). This is re-distilled (the *bonne chauffe*) and becomes Cognac. It must not contain above 72% alcohol, and this means that plenty of flavour is carried over from the wine.

Cognac is matured in oak casks in ground-floor stores called *chais*. Loss by evaporation, the 'angel's share', runs at an average 3% a year. At the annual stock-taking, casks are topped up with Brandy from slightly newer casks, thus building up average age. In the instance of very fine Cognac, when an average cask age of about fifty years has been achieved, the Cognac will no longer improve. This exceptional spirit is then transferred to glass containers and it can then be kept indefinitely; small quantities will be added to the finest Cognac blends sold by that particular house to improve the quality even further. (There is no such thing as 'vintage brandy' except for the now unusual instances where spirit is shipped a year after the vintage to mature in the importing country; in which case it may carry a year—that of the vintage. Nor does true Napoleon Cognac exist, except for rare collector's items.)

Cognac is a closely protected word and may only be applied to brandy made in a well defined area centring on the town of the same name. The Cognac region is subdivided into the Grande Champagne, the most prestigious, the Petite Champagne, and five bigger and less important districts. *Fine Champagne* is not a topographical designation but a legal description of Cognac Brandy distilled from the produce of the Grande and Petite Champagnes only, with not less than 50% from the former.

Quality 'Three Star' brandies, some having brand-names instead of stars, will be about 5 years old on average. A usual description of 'liqueur' Cognac is VSOP (Very Special Old Pale, or Superior), and above that most proprietors use various special names, plus accurate descriptions, like *fine Champagne*, for special grades.

Superior grades of Cognac are obviously only to be savoured neat. They are not for:

## Alexander

1 each Cognac; fresh cream; Crème de Cacao. Shake. Strain.

## Sidecar

1 Cognac; $\frac{1}{2}$ each lemon juice and Cointreau. Shake. Strain.

## Champagne Cocktail

In goblet place lump of sugar with 2 dashes Angostura; 1 Cognac; top with iced Dry Champagne.

# BEFORE A MEAL

*If Sherry makes you drowsy, and Whisky does not appeal to you, try some of the other appetisers which are light in texture and not too intoxicating. They make an excellent prelude to a meal because their delicate flavour doesn't overwhelm the taste-buds.*
*If on the other hand you need a pick-me-up, go for one of the Anis or Aquavit spirits.*

## VERMOUTHS

Vermouth is an extremely popular drink in Britain, and is most commonly taken straight and sweet, on and off the rocks, or as a mainstay to many cocktails. 'French' Vermouth is dry and white, and 'Italian' sweet and red, but the words have no specific geographical significance, because other wine-producing countries make both kinds.
Vermouth is blended according to strictly guarded formulae, but is basically wine infused with a variety of herbs and spices, and usually fortified with Brandy. Its origins are believed to date back to the fifth century BC: they may have been evolved in Ancient Greece by Hippocrates. The oldest known commercial producer is Carpano, who began producing his Vermouth in the eighteenth century, and the family is still going strong today. The word is believed to derive from the German *wermutwein*, the name for a highly-esteemed medicine, consisting of wine and wormwood.
There is a wide variety of brands available today, so it is best to try them all and then—since flavours differ quite considerably—choose the one most suited to your palate.

### Cinzano
Cinzano, with Martini and Rossi, is probably the most widely known brand name. The company is based in Turin, and in addition to the famous Bianco, also produces a world-renowned red. Half-and-half Cinzano Bianco and soda in a tall glass with a twist of lemon and lots of ice, makes a light, refreshing drink.
For a more decorative look, fill a glass with cracked ice, add red vermouth, a few

dashes of Curaçao, a teaspoon of sugar and stir. Add fruit, a sprig of mint and a couple of straws.

### Chambéry
Chambéry is probably the least known Vermouth, but it is quite outstanding—light, clear and fresh. Like many good things, it isn't easy to obtain, but certain specialist wine-shops do stock it. It comes from the Savoy Alps of France, and is a registered trade name. Of the four producers, the oldest is Dolin, founded in 1821, the producer, too, of Chambéryzette, a delicate dry Vermouth, flavoured with the juice of wild strawberries. (Another name to look for is Gaudin.) Like all Vermouths, it is best served well-chilled and will mix happily with gin, in whatever glass you care to choose. Other branded Vermouths to try are Dubonnet, St. Raphael and Lillet. Vermouths may be served however you enjoy them most, but are probably at their best in tall glasses, with lots of ice and a long twist of lemon peel. Add soda for a longer drink, or Vodka for extra verve.

### Punt e Mes
Punt e Mes is a deluxe Vermouth from Carpano of Turin. It has a distinctive bitter-sweet taste, and to my mind it is best served with ice and a slice of lemon in a long glass, although it gets along well with gin or soda. Its taste is clean and positive, and if you drink two or three, you won't feel drowsy after lunch.

## BITTERS

### Campari
Campari has rocketed in popularity quite recently. It is a Bitters, not a Vermouth, and with a British proof of 45° (US 50°) is classified by Customs and Excise as a spirit. It has a bitter-sweet taste, described aptly in advertisements as cryptic, is a rich pink in colour, and has a delicate bouquet.
It is made by macerating herbs in fortified wine, and is best served with ice and soda and a slice of orange. (The Italians serve it in 'one drink' Campari-Soda bottles, available in any café or restaurant.) If you like a really sharp flavour, try Campari with tonic—and insist on orange, not lemon. Half-and-half Campari and fresh orange juice—very cold—is delicious too.

### Angostura Bitters
It is worth mentioning Angostura Bitters just briefly here. It is good in Gin and water, and a few drops added to the water in your ice-cube tray will give the cubes a subtle fragrance that won't harm your Dry Martini in the least.

## KIR

An amazing drink for summer days is

Vin Blanc Cassis, or Kir, as it is sometimes called. It was invented by a Canon Kir, a former Mayor of Dijon. It is quite simply very cold Chablis mixed with Crème de Cassis—the blackcurrant liqueur, not the Sirop de Cassis—5 parts wine to one part Cassis.

## STRONGER APERITIFS AND SPIRITS

The next group of drinks are considerably more emphatic, and guaranteed to work on a drooping spirit like a powerful charm.

### Anis
Anis is the general name for a wide variety of Pastis, the aniseed- and liquorice-flavoured spirits, commonly associated with Marseilles.
Pernod is a soothing, subtle and exciting drink. It has many cousins all over the world with more or less the same qualities including, for example, Ouzo in Greece, Ojen in Spain, and some types of arrack. Pernod and Pastis are a sharp, clear yellow, the colour of lemonade powder, Ouzo is clear and colourless, and they all turn a milky white when cold water is added (about one part of Pernod, for example, to five parts water). A drink best taken from a long glass.

### Tequila
The traditional spirit of Mexico, Tequila is distilled from the fermented sap of the *maguey*, a cactus-type vegetable. The end-product is called *mezcal*—a firewater reputed to have hallucinatory side-effects. Tequila is a refined version of *mezcal*. The traditional way to drink it is with salt on the back of the hand, and a squeeze of fresh lemon juice.

### Aquavit
This is derived from the Latin Aqua Vitae, the term for distilled alcohol, and it applies to most Scandinavian spirits, flavoured or plain. They are best drunk with salt fish or the traditional smörgåsbord, but they go well with German food, too.
They are variously flavoured with fruit, except for Aalborg, which is clear and has a faint hint of caraway seeds.
The way to drink Aquavit is very, very cold, in small glasses, and swallowed in one quick gulp.

### Slivovitz
This comes into the same category as Aquavit. It is drunk widely in Central Europe and the Balkans, but is chiefly associated with Yugoslavia. It is basically plum brandy, and—a word of warning—its quality is very variable.

*Foreground: a measure of Pernod being topped up with five parts of water. Background: vermouths and bitters.*

# SUBTLE SHERRY

*Sherry and Madeira have many things in common. They are both fortified wines, strengthened by spirit so as to be rather stronger than table wines, about 17%-21% alcohol.*

Both come from southern latitudes, yet their vineyards fall within the moderating influence of the Atlantic, so that they have subtlety and delicacy. They are both great wines and they are both grossly underrated. Their flavours are wonderfully deep and complex. Both are available in a wide range of sweetness. But here the difference between them begins to show, for the driest Sherries are much drier than the driest Madeiras—indeed they are bone dry— and the sweetest Sherries are sweeter. Both can live, in the cask and in the bottle, to attain great age. But here, too, there are differences. Although vintage Sherries are occasionally made, they are rarely sold commercially. Vintage Madeiras, however, *are* available—but not many and generally only the oldest vintages, which are very expensive—and worth their price. In practice, both are matured on the *solera* system, which works like this: if a shipper has a cask of wine of a style which he particularly likes he draws off a proportion of it (perhaps a third), filling the void with a younger wine of the same style. After a time, the young wine will take on the character of the old and the shipper will be back where he started. This can be done over several stages, creating a complete system, one cask feeding another, so that the youngest receives newly fermented wine while the oldest gives wine with all the characteristics of great age. So, years and vineyards do not matter: the style and quality stay the same. But here a word of warning: if a wine is labelled 'Solera 1850', this does not mean that it is an 1850 wine. All that it means is that the solera was created in 1850. It will contain an infinitesimally small amount of 1850 wine, but it need be no older in style than one started in 1950.

## SHERRY

Sherry is flattered by having many imitators, some of them very good wines. But genuine *Sherry* only comes from Spain: to be precise, from Andalusia, around the old, delightful town of Jerez de la Frontera, known to the Arabs as Scheris, from which the English word and the modern Spanish word are both derived.

There are two basic kinds: *fino* and *oloroso*. Both come from the same grapes grown in the same vineyards. Which kind the wine turns out to be is largely a matter of chance. The wine makes up its own mind. If it turns out to be fino a strange thing happens: a layer of yeast cells grows on its surface. Called the *flor*, it does much to give it its flavour and style, with a unique, very penetrating aroma. Oloroso is darker and somewhat heavier, and although its name in Spanish means 'fragrant', its aroma is deep and mellow, less assertive than that of a fino. Both kinds are bone dry. To make a sweet Sherry, specially prepared sweetening wines have to be added. While those are the two basic kinds of Sherry, there are many variants. *Manzanilla* is a special kind of fino, matured in the sea air at Sanlucar de Barrameda on the mouth of the Guadalquivir. It is very dry and fresh with a salt tang to it. As fino ages, its character changes subtly; it grows darker in colour and acquires a flavour and aroma generally described as 'nutty'. Indeed it comes rather to resemble the wines of Montilla, grown in the hills near Cordova, and hence its name: *amontillado*. The term is one that is widely misused, to the extent that some merchants seem to think that it is synonymous with 'medium-dry Sherry' A real amontillado is an old wine. It is therefore necessarily expensive and it is well worth paying for. It can be absolutely bone dry but is usually sweetened to some extent. An *amoroso* is a lightish style of oloroso with a fair degree of sweetness. *Cream Sherries*, being so fashionable, vary considerably in quality and style. They are generally lighter and sweeter than amorosos. *Brown Sherries* are dark, heavy olorosos made very sweet. And there are several other styles which are found from time to time.

### How to serve Sherry

Fino Sherry is best served chilled, but not frozen stiff. About 10°C (50°F) is ideal. Amontillados and medium Sherries generally taste best very slightly chilled. Olorosos are normally best at room temperature.

As part of the joy of Sherry lies in its superb fragrance, *all* Sherry should be served in large glasses. Copitas are best: those tall, narrow glasses that are widest near the bottom and gradually taper inwards towards the top, where the concentrated fragrance can gather. Failing a copita, a good tulip-shaped wine glass will do just as well. Neither should be more than one third full.

In contact with the air, Sherry oxidizes The deterioration in a fino or other dry wine can be seen easily after only two or three days, though a fino kept cool at a steady 10°C (50°F) in a refrigerator will last twice as long. Medium Sherries last longer and sweet Sherries for a few weeks. Normally this is academic as they soon get drunk. But if they don't, there are two remedies: buy half bottles or, as soon as a bottle is opened, decant half of it into a spare half bottle and cork it tightly. Then it will last as long as if it had never been opened.

Another thing to remember is that fino Sherry does not like bottles. Once bottled, it deteriorates slowly but steadily and is never quite at its best even after as little as three months. So buy it in small quantities from an outlet with a quick turnover. However, amontillado Sherries and medium Sherries generally are happy for several years in bottles. Sweet olorosos actually improve. Their sweetness gradually and mysteriously gets eaten away and the wines take on a special character of aroma that is all their own. These Sherries with 'bottle age' are prized by connoisseurs. But to make it worthwhile they have to be kept for at least ten years.

### Montilla

Having mentioned Montilla, I should say a little more. The area now known as Montilla-Moriles was considered an outlying part of the Sherry district until the early 1930s, when it was hived off by a meticulous government. The decree was, perhaps, right as the wines do have a character of their own which is not quite like Sherry, though there are the same styles of fino and oloroso. There is even a montilla-amontillado: an example of rendering unto Caesar the thing that is Caesar's. Because they are less well known than Sherry, these wines are generally cheaper and are well worth looking out for. They are served in the same way as Sherry.

### MADEIRA

Madeira comes from Madeira and, happily, can come from nowhere else, as its name is one of the only two that is directly protected by law—the other being Port. A unique feature about it is the way it is matured, using *estufas*, or hot rooms, in which the wines are gradually heated to about 49°C (120°F) over a period of about a month, left at that temperature for about four months, and then cooled over another month. It is this that gives them their unique and

delicious, slightly burnt flavour. The four most popular kinds are named after the vines that produce them: *sercial, verdelho, bual* and *malmsey*. There are two other descriptions that are sometimes found, especially in America: south side and rainwater. The former is a rich blend, like malmsey. The latter is drier, more like a sercial. The drier kinds of madeira—sercial and verdelho—are generally preferred slightly chilled as aperitifs and the sweeter ones—bual and malmsey—as dessert wines. Madeira has one very real advantage over Sherry: it does not mind being bottled and oxidizes much more slowly after being opened, so that there is not much deterioration even after several weeks.

## TAPAS

A final word. In the bars of Jerez, Sherry is served with *tapas*—small snacks. It tastes best that way, wherever it is drunk, and so does Madeira. *Tapas* need not be elaborate—a slice of salami is ideal, or some olives, nuts, slivers of cheese, or potato crisps. Both Sherry and Madeira taste excellent, too, when taken with a course in a meal. Apart from the soup, a fino Sherry tastes well with fish, especially shellfish or oysters, and a sweet Sherry or Madeira is ideal with a pudding.

## FORTIFIED WINES FROM OTHER COUNTRIES

True Sherry only comes from Spain, but many other countries produce similar fortified wines which emulate the Spanish types of Sherry, notably South Africa and Australia. In America, California produces quite a range of sherry-type wines with a somewhat nutty flavour, ranging from dark to light amber in colour, dry to sweet in flavour.

*Top left: a Sherry Bodega (or store). Top right: wine skins in Madeira. Below: copitas of Sherry. From left to right – Fino, Amontillado, a blend of Oloroso and Amontillado, Oloroso, and Brown.*

## TYPES OF SHERRY

**Fino:** light in colour, body and style: penetrating aroma; very dry
**Manzanilla:** a form of fino; very dry and fresh, with a salty tang
**Amontillado:** fino aged to a darker colour, nutty flavour and aroma; can be very dry but usually sweetened
**Oloroso:** darker and heavier than fino; usually sweetened.
**Amoroso:** a lightish oloroso, fairly sweet
**Cream Sherry:** lighter and sweeter than amoroso
**Brown Sherry:** a dark, heavy oloroso; very sweet

# WHAT TO DRINK WITH WHAT...

*It can all really be said in a few words: red wine with meat, white wine with fish, rosé when in doubt, and Champagne when extravagant. Just drink the wine and enjoy it. The only way to find out what you like is to keep on experimenting and there are certainly no rigid rules to follow. But you may find that the suggestions on the next six pages gives you some new ideas. Use them one of two ways–either choose a dish and see if the wine paired with it inspires you, or start with the drink and match a dish to it. If you're planning a dinner party, a helpful wine merchant should be able to suggest what to drink with it—if you're in a restaurant, any wine waiter worth his salt should make recommendations—and not all from the most expensive wines on his list !*

The more you know, the more interesting wine becomes. The basic ideas have grown up through experiment, and have subsequently become tradition for extremely good reasons. Red wine doesn't go well with white fish because this seems to bring out a rather metallic, tinny taste in the wine, whereas the flavour of the white wine is complemented by that of the fish. This is the main object—to choose a wine that makes a perfect partnership with the food. Of course, some wines are absolutely perfect drunk by themselves, and it is a waste to cloud their taste with any food at all!

## TRADITIONAL MEALS

A full formal meal can have Champagne as an aperitif, Sherry with the soup, dry white wine with fish, Claret or Burgundy with red meat or game, sweet white wine or sweet sparkling wine with pudding; Port with the cheese and Brandy and liqueurs after the meal. Fortunately (or maybe unfortunately) that doesn't happen too often now. If you are having a fairly straightforward meal and want one wine to serve right through, make sure it does go reasonably with the various dishes.
Having a large jug of iced water on the table is a good American custom; it seems odd, but wine does make one terribly thirsty. A glass of mineral water is good as a thirst-quencher, too.

## ORDER OF SERVING

There is a general rule to follow if you are interested in showing the wines to their best advantage: young before old; dry before sweet; white before red, or before sweet white; good wine before great.

## APPROPRIATE WINE

Apart from matching the wine to the food and the occasion, choose it with the company in mind, too. Don't give a really good wine to people who will drink it like orange squash, if this is going to annoy you.

## CHOOSING IN A RESTAURANT

Choosing wine in a restaurant seems to present more of a problem than buying it for home use. Perhaps it's because wine waiters tend to hover about rather impatiently. If you can't remember what any of the wines taste like, don't think it mean to order half bottles. It gives a perfect opportunity for finding out what more wines are like, and you can always re-order. Half bottles are not supposed to be as good for producing the perfect wine as whole ones—a magnum is even better, but most of us can't afford magnums all the time.
There are all sorts of things that go better than wine with the particular dishes of their own country: Schnapps with herring, Retsina or Ouzo with taramasalata, for example. Guinness goes with mussels and Hock and Seltzer with strawberries, but one can mix and match all sorts of things to make a change.
If there are two of you, the usual practice is to order half a bottle of dryish white wine to go with the first course and a whole bottle of red or white for the second. However, one bottle may well last the whole meal, depending on your thirst. Champagne goes perfectly throughout a meal. For a touch of glamour at half the price try half a bottle as an aperitif and to drink with the first course.

When in doubt the carafe wine is naturally the safest bet, though, sadly, it's not always as good as it should be. It is a good indication of a restaurant's standards if the patron has chosen a sound carafe wine. It is definitely the answer for a large party, when everyone has ordered totally different dishes. Red, white and rosé are usually listed, and some more enterprising restaurants have a choice of both sweet and dry white.

## COMPARING WINES

Of course, there are hundreds and hundreds of wines to choose from. One cannot possibly list them all. Some particular favourites may be missed out, and anyway, once you do start trying to find your own personal choice to go with different dishes, the game is endless. The best place to experiment is at home. It's much cheaper than paying restaurant mark ups for what might be a BIG mistake. At least at home you can open another bottle and keep The Mistake to drink at the next meal with something better suited to it.
It is mostly French and German wines that are listed in the recommendations at the end of this chapter because they have come to be known and accepted as the best wines of their particular type throughout the world. That is not to say that many other countries do not also produce excellent wines, even though they don't have the wonderful finesse and bouquet of a Lafite or Latour. Sadly, some of the better French and German wines are becoming so exorbitant that one is forced to try other wines, apart from the interest of doing so, if meals are not going to become ruinously expensive. One can't have a Margaux with every meal—but who, truthfully, would want to. Half the joy of appreciating the best is knowing the ordinary.

### A memory for taste

If French wines are hard to get, or very expensive in your part of the world, try one just occasionally. It will give you a standard by which to measure the wines that are more readily available. When you have made comparisons and discovered the wines you particularly enjoy, you can start to build up your own personal list. The only thing is to drink as many wines as possible and try to remember what they taste like. This is probably the most difficult part—to actually build up an accurate taste memory. It does not seem to come so naturally as remembering colours or sounds, perhaps because people are not generally brought up to describe and record the taste in words. They simply drink. Happily!

## SPECIAL NATIONAL FOOD

### Curry

One of the guide-lines is to match the style of cooking of the country or the area with the wine. In an Italian restaurant you can hardly avoid drinking Italian wine, but this approach doesn't work when it comes to an Indian restaurant. Curry is difficult to match because the hot spiciness completely overpowers any other flavour, and frequently leaves one gasping. Lager is the most popular choice. A spicy Alsace Gewürtztraminer or a strong Rhône wine go quite well, but in the end most of the taste is quite obscured anyway; lime juice and soda water is far cheaper.

### Chinese Food

The Chinese is the only other great cuisine in the world to match that of the French, in the variety of dishes and sauces from all over the vast continent, but China has never produced very good wine. Selecting what to drink with Chinese food is very much a matter of personal taste; there are no really good guide-lines to follow, not even from the Chinese I have asked. Try a strong Hock, a Burgundy or, again, a Rhône. Italian wines go best, I think, but there are so many small dishes in the course of a Chinese meal that it is quite impossible to find something that matches all the delicate flavours. Chinese tea is delicious—and infinitely more refreshing than coffee at the end of the meal.

## THE WINES OF DIFFERENT COUNTRIES

Italy has almost as large a range and variety as France, and her wines are now much more dependable in standard than they once were. Switzerland produces wines with an absolutely distinct aroma and taste and I rather like them. The Dôle from the Pinot Noir and Gamay grape is characteristically velvety and the white wines are extremely dry, some with a very flinty taste. Naturally the wine for fondu. These Swiss wines are rare and expensive, too, since the difficulties in growing the wine prohibit the making of large quantities, and most of what is produced is drunk locally. The light white Vinho Verdes from Portugal are perfect for picnics; and a

*A bottle of wine will improve almost any meal one hundred per cent – whether you're planning an informal meal based on a great big dish of Paella for a Sunday lunch or are going out to dinner in a restaurant.*

famous rosé has put Portuguese table wines on the lists all over the world. There should be more reasonably-priced wines from Portugal as it develops its potential.

Austrian wines make a change with summer dishes, lunch or dinner. A popular table wine brought these wines further to the fore, as it did in Portugal. Austrian white wines are best, Apetlon and Schluck, and the spicey Grüner Veltliner.

From Middle and Eastern Europe there are dozens of different tastes to try for weekend and lunchtime drinking. The best wines are mainly white: Chardonnay from Bulgaria, Cotnari from Romania, and from Hungary the sweet white dessert wine, Tokay. Yugoslav Riesling needs no introduction as an excellent medium-priced white wine.

Cyprus made its name with Sherry, but is now producing in quantity some table wines that are being shipped to England. The white wines are rather sweet, with an underlying bitterness and hardly any 'finish' at all, due to a lack of the acidity one finds in German wines. They make inexpensive everyday wines.

Lastly Spain, which produces much better quality wines in the Rioja district than was once upon a time admitted. Chile also produces excellent red wines at splendid value. Wines from South Africa, Australia and California are all available, too, but because of the distance they have to travel, they are not so economical.

# MATCHING WINES AND DISHES

Many wines will go with every dish. In most cases there are really no hard and fast rules, and where there are, it's a good idea to try something different. It largely depends on how much you feel like spending and, if you're at home, what wine you've got in stock.

## Hors d'Oeuvre

In principle, the hors d'oeuvre is death to any wine. The vinegar is a direct enemy. In French *vin aigre* means sour wine, and the two just do not mix. That is not to say that you can't drink anything, but don't expect it to taste its best and then wonder why it doesn't. Whatever you were drinking as aperitif goes quite well (but not whisky or gin). Smoked salmon and eel are difficult as the oily taste is so strong. But most of the 'starters' on a basic menu go best with a dry white wine. With oysters the accepted choice is Chablis or Muscadet. Some gamey patés are better with Burgundy, and Quiche Lorraine naturally goes with the wine of its country—Alsace. In grapefruit the acidity destroys any other taste.

## Soup

Sherry is the best accompaniment for clear soup, and if it is not desperately expensive, tastes delicious actually in the soup. A wine is not generally chosen to match this course, so just start with whatever wine you've chosen for the main course.

## Eggs

Eggs do not go with any wines particularly well. The sulphur in them somehow flattens the taste of the wine altogether. *Ouefs en cocotte* is blander than some egg dishes, but it's better to start the wine when you've finished the egg.

## Fish

Fish can be divided into as many categories as meat, all with their own styles and sauces. If the cooking is simple, then a medium dry white; if the sauce is rich then a stronger flavoured wine. The really superb Burgundies, the Rhine and Moselle wines, these complement any dish that has had a great deal of work put into it. A very strong wine with something like a plain *Truite au Bleu* will simply overpower the delicate flavour and it is rather a waste of both wine and food. Loire wines are excellent. If you want an interesting variation in tastes from the same area, compare a Muscadet with a Sancerre. The former is light and crisp and the latter has a flinty taste and a very strong bouquet. Salmon and lobster deserve individual attention. Opinion varies on what goes best with them: some people prefer a fine premier cru Claret with hot salmon. With lobster try Hock, Alsace or a very good Beaujolais.

## Meat—white meat, pork or veal

Either red wine or a white wine that is not too dry and there are no hard-and-fast rules; a large number of wines go very well. It all depends on the nationality of the restaurant, and how much you feel like spending.

## Meat—red meat, lamb or beef

Red wines: I prefer Claret with lamb and a Burgundy or Rhône with beef. An Italian Barolo is a different wine to try; it has several years of bottle age. There are also some good claret-type wines from Torgiano, the central area of Italy. If you have mint sauce, don't expect that to do anything for the wine. A strong Rhône will counteract it fairly well.

## Birds—chicken and turkey

Chicken is a very versatile bird, lending itself to all sorts of marvellous sauces, and the wine should follow the style of the dish. With a *coq au vin*, for example, a wine from the Burgundy area; with Chicken Parisiènne, Champagne; with plain roast chicken, a good Claret, and so on.

Turkey also goes with Claret or white wine.

## Game

Pheasant, grouse, partridge, quail, pigeon and hare all call for a red wine. The higher the game is hung, the stronger the wine should be. Venison goes well with a Côte Rôtie or Hermitage from the Rhône, and also with a very good Rhine wine, which is not so surprising, perhaps, when one remembers how many deer there are in Germany. The local wine is the natural partner.

## Cheese

Port or, if you don't like Port, red wine. With Bel Paese a vintage Chianti, with Brie a Burgundy.

## Pudding

Wine does not like the acid in fruit, so a good wine should be chosen if you are selecting something specially for this course. The maxim of the wine merchant is to buy on apples and sell on cheese. Sometimes two really sweet flavours together are too much, but a sweet Sauterne with peaches can be delicious, and so can a Tawny Port with ice cream, or the Madeiras and Muscatels. The really superb German Trockenbeerenauslese or Château Yquem, for example, should be drunk quite alone, preferably on a terrace on a perfect summer evening.

## Coffee

Port, Brandy, Armagnac, Malt Whisky or any of the dozens of liqueurs on the market.

## Picnics

When you are travelling abroad, obviously the best choice is the local *vin du pays*. The wine can be kept cool either by being part-buried in the earth, or put in a stream if there happens to be one handy. Don't forget to anchor it firmly, otherwise your last sight of the bottle may be as it bobs gently downstream.

P.S. A thoughtful idea for a birthday party if you can afford it: if the year was a good one, and if it will be appreciated, choose a wine of the same vintage as the person whose birthday it is.

*Above left: Fondu being a traditional Swiss dish, it would be fitting to drink a red Swiss wine, like Dole, with it. Otherwise, try a Claret. Above right: Nasi Goreng, from Indonesia, is best accompanied by Lager (as is curry). Below: red wines are usually preferred with roasts of beef or lamb.*

# ...AND HERE ARE SOME SUGGESTIONS

*The following suggestions are* not *rules, just some ideas to try. (Red or white wine may go equally well with several dishes.) If you're not in Europe, experiment with as many locally-available versions as possible.*

## STARTERS

| | |
|---|---|
| **Honeydew Melon** | ENGLAND: *Adgetstone Estate* |
| **Consommé** | SPAIN: *Dry Sherry* |
| **Soufflé** | AUSTRIA: *Schluck* |
| **Pâté** | BURGUNDY: *Beaune* |
| **Oeuf en Cocotte** | BURGUNDY: *Bourgogne Aligoté* |
| **Gaspacho Andaluz** | SPAIN: *Rioja Red* |
| **Prawn Cocktail** | LOIRE: *Muscadet* |
| **Spaghetti Bolognese** | ITALY: *Chianti* |
| **Spaghetti alla Vongole** | ITALY: *Verdicchio dei Castelli Jesi* |
| **Quiche Lorraine** | ALSACE: *Traminer* |
| **Cold Borscht** | HUNGARY: *Rosé Magyar* |
| **Taramasalata** | GREECE: *Retsina* |
| **Artichokes** | BURGUNDY: *Mâcon, Chablis* |
| **Avocados** | BORDEAUX: *Graves* |
| **Fish Dishes** | LOIRE: *Muscadet, Vouvray* |
| **Egg Dishes** | PORTUGAL: *Vinho Verde* |
| **Parma Ham** | BULGARIA: *Chardonnay* |
| **Snails** | ITALY: *Frascati, Soave, Verdicchio* |
| | GERMANY: *Rhine or Moselle* |

## SOUP

| | |
|---|---|
| **Clear Soup** | *Sherry, Madeira* |
| **Lobster Bisque** | *Dry White* |
| **Meat Soups** | *Red* |
| **Vichysoisse** | ALSACE: *Muscat d'Alsace* |

## FISH AND SEAFOOD (WHITE)

| | |
|---|---|
| **Fish with Sauces** | *Finer Premier Cru wines* |
| **Oysters** | *Champagne, Chablis, or Guinness* |
| **Smoked Salmon** | LOIRE: *Sancerre* |
| **Moules Marinière** | LOIRE: *Gros Plant du Pays Nantais* |
| **Dressed Crab** | LOIRE: *Saumur Blanc de Blancs* |
| **Trout** | GERMANY: *Berkasteler Doktor,* |
| **Truite au Bleu** | LOIRE: *Pouilly Blanc Fumé* |
| **Smoked Eel** | ITALY: *Frascati* |
| **Sole** | BURGUNDY: *Meursaults* |
| **Sole Meunière** | GERMANY: *Moselle Piesporter, Michelsberg Natur* |
| **Scampi Provençale** | RHONE: *Tavel Rosé* |
| **Poached Salmon** | BURGUNDY: *Le Montrachet* |
| **Cold Salmon Mayonnaise** | LOIRE: *Muscadet* |
| **Grilled Herrings** | YUGOSLAVIA: *Riesling* |
| **Quenelles de Brochet** | LOIRE: *Sauvignon* |
| **Soused Herrings** | SCANDINAVIA: *Schnapps* |
| **Kedgeree** | HUNGARY: *Magyar Pecs Riesling* |
| **Caviar** | POLAND: *Vodka* |
| **Turbot** | BURGUNDY: *Le Montrachet* |
| **Turbot au Gratin** | SWITZERLAND: *Fendant de Sion* |

| | |
|---|---|
| **Lobster in Pernod** | FRANCE: *Pastis* |
| **Japanese Tempura** | JAPAN: *Saki* |
| **Coquilles St. Jacques a la Bretonne** | BURGUNDY: *Mâcon Villages* |
| **Fish and Chips** | *Guinness* |
| **John Dory** | SWITZERLAND: *Dorin* |
| **Red Mullet** | GERMAN: *Spätlese and Auslese wines* |
| **Shellfish** | LOIRE: *Pouilly Fumé, Sancerre* |
| | ALSACE: *Gewürtztraminer* |
| | SOUTH AFRICA: *Twee Jongegezellen, Paarl Steen, Nederburg Riesling* |
| | AUSTRALIA: *Barossa Rhine Riesling, Hunter Valley Blanquette* |
| | AUSTRIA: *Grüner Veltliner, Schluck* |
| **Kippers** | *Red or white Provence* |
| **Fruits de mer** | LANGUEDOC: *Clairette du Languedoc* |
| | PROVENCE: *Bandol, Palette.* |

## PASTA

| | |
|---|---|
| | *Strong red wines* |
| | ITALY: *Chianti, Corvo, Valpolicella* |
| | SPAIN: *Rioja* |

## MEAT

| | |
|---|---|
| **White meat** | *Light red or medium dry white* |
| **VEAL** | |
| **Roast Veal** | ITALY: *Barolo, Torgiano* |
| | GERMANY: *Bernkasteler Riesling* |
| **Veal Fricandeau a l'Oseille** | LANGUEDOC: *Rosé Pelure d'Oignon* |
| **Osso Bucco** | ITALY: *Barbaresco* |
| **Weiner Schnitzel** | AUSTRIA: *Grüner Veltliner* |
| **Saltimbocca** | ITALY: *Valpolicella* |
| **PORK AND HAM** | |
| **Roast Pork** | BEAUJOLAIS: *Morgon, Fleurie* |
| **Pork Chops in Cider** | NORMANDY: *Cider* |
| **Ham in Madeira Sauce** | SICILY: *Corvo* |
| **Jambon Persillé** | BURGUNDY: *Beaujolais Nouveau* |
| **Rillettes de Tours** | LOIRE: *Touraine Cabernet Rosé* |
| **Grilled Gammon and Cloves** | RHONE: *Crozes Hermitage (R)* |
| **Sucking Pig** | CLARET: *Château Batailley (Pauillac)* |
| **LAMB AND MUTTON** | |
| **Roast Leg of Lamb** | COTE DE BEAUNE: *Aloxe Corton, Volnay, Santenay* |
| | SPAIN: *Good Rioja* |

| | |
|---|---|
| **Roast Rack of Lamb** | CLARET: *Château Leoville Lascases (St. Julien) '66* |
| **Carre d'Agneau** | CLARET: *Château Pontet Canet (Pauillac) '66* |
| **Lamb Cutlets** | BEAUJOLAIS: *Moulin à Vent* |
| **Navarin of Mutton** | BURGUNDY: *Aloxe Corton* |

**BEEF (RED)**

| | |
|---|---|
| **Roast Beef and Yorkshire Pudding** | CLARET: *Château Talbot (St. Julien)* |
| **Boeuf Stroganoff** | BULGARIA: *Chardonnay* |
| **Goulash** | HUNGARY: *Bull's Blood of Eger* |
| **Steak au Poivre** | ARGENTINA: *Rosado* |
| | CHILE: *Cabernet* |
| **Hamburgers** | ALGERIA: *Red* |
| **Salt Brisket** | ALSACE: *Sylvaner* |
| **Steak Tartare** | *Aquavit* |
| **Fondue Bourguignonne** | BURGUNDY: *Gevrey-Chambertin, Chambolle-Musigny, Vosne-Romanée* |

**CHICKEN AND POULTRY (RED OR WHITE)**

| | |
|---|---|
| **Coq au Vin** | BURGUNDY: *Chambolle Musigny* |
| **Chicken Kiev** | BURGUNDY: *Volnay* |
| **Roast Chicken** | CLARET: *Château Rausan Segla (Margaux) '61* |
| **Chicken Fricassé** | BURGUNDY: *Puligny Montrachet* |
| **Roast Turkey** | BURGUNDY: *Vosne Romanée* |
| **Roast Duck** | LOIRE: *Chinon, Bourgueil* |
| | ITALY: *Valpolicella, Barbera* |
| | RHONE: *Côte Rôtie* |
| **Salmis of Duck** | RHONE: *Châteauneuf du Pape* |
| **Roast Goose** | HOCK: *Marcobrunner Riesling, Spätlese* |

**GAME (RED)**

| | |
|---|---|
| **Roast Pheasant** | CLARET: *Château Gruaud Larose (St. Julien)* |
| **Civet de Lievre** | CLARET: *Château Cheval Blanc (St. Emilion)* |
| **Casseroled Partridge** | CLARET: *Château Lynch Bages (Pauillac)* |
| **Rabbit Pie** | BEAUJOLAIS: *Vin de l'Année* |
| **Roast Grouse** | BURGUNDY: *Grands Echezeaux. Domaine de la Romanée-Conti* |
| **Pigeon with Cherries** | PORTUGAL: *Marquis de Soveral* |
| **Quail en Caisses** | CLARET: *Château Troplong Mondot* |
| **Terrine of Hare** | RHONE: *St. Joseph* |
| **Roast Haunch of Venison** | HOCK: *Schloss Vollrads* |

**GENERAL**

| | |
|---|---|
| **Bubble and Squeak** | CHILE: *Cabernet* |
| **Tripe and Onions** | MOROCCO: *Vin Rouge* |
| **Haggis** | SCOTLAND: *Malt Whisky, Scotch Ale* |
| **Irish Stew** | BEAUJOLAIS: *Fleurie Blanc* |
| **Steak and Kidney Pudding** | BURGUNDY: *Mâcon* |
| **Liver and Bacon** | PORTUGUESE: *Rosé* |
| **Eggs, Bacon, Chips, Sausages, etc.** | *Anything you fancy—wine, Guinness, beer, cider* |

**ORIENTAL DISHES**

| | |
|---|---|
| **Tandoori Chicken** | ALSACE: *Gewürztztraminer* |
| **Madras Curry** | GERMANY: *Holsten Pilsner* |
| **Peking Duck** | ITALY: *Soave* |
| **Shish Kebab** | YUGOSLAVIA: *Lutomer Riesling* |

**PICNICS**

| | |
|---|---|
| **Salads, Sandwiches** | RHONE: *Pouilly Fumé. Cider* |

**CHEESE**

| | |
|---|---|
| **Stilton** | PORTUGAL: *Vintage Port* |
| **Brie** | BURGUNDY: *Hospices de Beaune, Cuvée Nicholas Rolin* |
| **Roquefort** | BURGUNDY: *Ruchottes Chambertin* |
| **English Cheddar** | BURGUNDY: *Morey St. Denis* |
| **Bel Paese** | ITALY: *Umbria Torgiano* |
| **Welsh Rarebit** | BEER: *Best Bitter* |
| **Cheese Soufflé** | HOCK: *Niersteiner Domtal* |
| **Mild Cheeses—like Caerphilly** | *Claret* |

**PUDDINGS**

| | |
|---|---|
| **Strawberries and Cream** | *Champagne Demi Sec* |
| **Treacle Tart** | LOIRE: *Coteaux du Layon* |
| **Christmas Pudding** | MOSELLE: *Piesporter Goldtropfchen, Spätlese* |
| **Vanilla Ice Cream** | SHERRY: *Walnut Brown* |
| **Peaches** | PIEDMONT: *Asti Spumante* |
| **Zabaglione** | SICILY: *Marsala* |
| **Rice Pudding** | MOSELLE: *Graacher Himmelreich Riesling* |
| **Coffee Mousse** | LIQUEUR: *Tia Maria* |
| **Crepe Suzette** | LIQUEUR: *Grand Marnier* |
| **Apple Pie** | LOIRE: *Quarts de Chaume or Muscadet* |

# AN INTRODUCTION TO WINE

*The terminology of wine can be very off-putting, since most of it is in French. The air of mystery and complexity which this gives to one of the most important advances in human civilization puts up an artificial barrier between the wine and the drinker in a non-wine-growing country. So, avoiding as much as possible any suggestion of a 'lecture' on wines and wine-making, here, first, is a crib to help with understanding terms in common use, and then some basic information about wine labels.*

## WINE LORE

A great deal of rubbish has been written about wine. Wine is like music—describing it in words means very little. The experience of other people is not much help but, in fact, understanding it for yourself is quite easy. What we hope this book will do is provide something for you to refer to as you broaden your knowledge by experiment, and perhaps tempt you to try things that are unfamiliar or that you have previously ignored. The basic fact about wine is that it is for each individual to decide what wine he or she really enjoys and to go on enjoying it, regardless of whether it is supposed to 'go' with this dish or that.

In the past, people could rely on a knowledgeable and friendly wine-merchant to advise them, but now, with the growing number of chain-stores and supermarkets, and of less experienced merchants, it is wise to understand the rudiments for oneself.

## WHERE TO BEGIN

To start with a delicate dry wine is rather like being thrown in at the deep end before you can swim—it could put you off for life. Gradual progress from elementary wines opens the way to all manner of delight through the nose, eyes and palate until that serene state has been reached where all wines can be treated as old and valued friends.

The dryest white wines are likely to come from France—Burgundy (Aligoté and Mâcon Blanc to name the cheapest, with Pouilly Fuissé and the Montrachets going up the scale) or the Loire (Muscadet, Sancerre and Pouilly Fumé among them). In Germany Moselle wines are liable to be lighter in colour and alcohol, and fresher than Hocks; and in the French reds, Burgundy rather heavier than Claret, Rhône wines such as Côte du Rhône and Châteauneuf du Pape higher in alcoholic content than most other reds, the Dão wines of Portugal darker in colour than those from Spain's Rioja. The term 'dry' cannot properly be used in connection with red wine.

## BOTTLE SHAPES

Some wines may be identified by the shapes, and the colours of the bottles. Bordeaux bottles have well-defined 'shoulders' and are green for red wine, clear for white.

The standard Burgundy bottle has no shoulders and a bigger body than the Claret bottle, usually green. The Burgundy bottle is similar to the Champagne bottle but much lighter, in weight not colour. There is also a slightly smaller Burgundy bottle called Mâconnais, and the Pichet, which looks rather like an Indian club, best known for Beaujolais from the growers Piat or Mommesin.

Champagne bottle—heaviest of all because it has to be really sturdy to withstand the pressure from within from carbonic gas—a consideration which applies to other sparkling wines such as Germany's Sekt and Italy's Spumante. Alsace wine bottles—long necks and thin bodies.

Provence bottles—wasp-waisted like Edwardian ladies of fashion.

German wine bottles—similar to those of Alsace.

The white wines of Franconia (Germany) come in a traditional *bocksbutel*, a flask which has been adapted to contain the bubbles of sparkling Portuguese Mateus Rosé, and its Vinho Verde companion, Casal Garcia. You can scarcely mistake a Chianti bottle, with its bowl shape and wicker skirt, but many Italian wines (including Chiantis) are in bottles almost identical with those of France—a Bardolino in what looks like a Bordeaux bottle, for instance. Other countries, too, use French- and German-type bottles for wines of similar style, i.e. 'Spanish Burgundy' and 'South African Hock' and 'Champagne' from California.

## HOW MUCH IN A BOTTLE?

The contents of Hock and Moselle bottles are normally rather less (24 fluid oz, 6 decilitres) than of others—a bottle of Burgundy, for instance, usually consists of 26⅔ fluid oz (6½ decilitres), regarded here as the standard bottle size. On the subject of bottle sizes, Victor Lanson, head of the family providing the Champagne of that name, once said to me: 'A magnum is a suitable measure to be shared by two gentlemen'. A joke, yet M. Lanson has much respect for the magnum as a vessel, not only because the wine will be all the better for that extra quantity of wine, but because the wine will be all the better for that extra space in which to live and burgeon. Unfortunately for the consumer, the magnum bottle is rather more expensive to make so that it costs rather more than the two bottles which yield the equivalent content. A magnum of Champagne holds 1.60 litres, a magnum of Claret 1.50 litres. A demie, or half bottle of Champagne holds 40 centilitres, a demie of Claret 37.5 centilitres.

Bottles bigger than a magnum do not help the wine and are regarded as rather gimmicky, for show purposes only.

Half bottles are less popular than they once were and there are wine lovers who suspect them of cramping the wine so that it might not be quite as good as the same wine in a full-size bottle. Nevertheless, they have their uses, for dining alone or perhaps *à deux*—starting with white and following with a red, or just contrasting two different wines.

Many of us are now getting accustomed to the litre and double litre bottles. Most of the wine in bottles of these sizes is in the ordinaire class which will normally keep for a day or two, even several days, if recorked after use.

## BUYING A WINE

Buying wine for the home falls roughly into three categories, (1) Wine for everyday drinking—and the numbers of people who like a glass or two with the evening meal are soaring; (2) Wine for special occasions, such as dinner parties; and (3) Wine for laying down (and if you have not the facilities many merchants will store it for you at little cost).

The choice in the first category is ever widening. Austria, Spain, Italy, Portugal, Chile, Hungary and Yugoslavia and especially Spain, produce wines which are often cheaper than those of France and Germany. From the English-speaking world there are the excellent wines of Australia and South

Africa, the United States and Canada. Some wine is bottled by the château (or domaine) and others by the shipper. There is a higher mark-up on château-bottled wine than on wines bottled by the shipper in the country of sale because of costs of transporting the bottles.

**Cheap table wines**

Some of the most consistent *ordinaires*, to be sure, come from France and may still be found at most reasonable prices—a pitcher containing approximately three bottles is about as cheap a party 'buy' as you will find. Whatever the source, it can be said that those wines imported in bulk and bottled under the labels of the big supermarket chains—in such quantities that they can be sold cheaply —do represent value for money. Most of them are adequately described so that choice is made easy. And do not be afraid to blend, say a sweetish red with one much drier, to arrive at a wine to suit your taste.

**Wine for dinner**

For special occasions, a vintage Claret or Burgundy from France will not only embellish the meal but flatter the guests. Clarets of 1961 and 1966 are outstanding, red Burgundies of 1962 and 1964 are very good indeed and the whites of 1962 exceptional. Champagne before the meal is my top choice (again a compliment to the guests) with a white Burgundy or a Loire wine (or a Hock or Moselle if you want something a trifle sweeter) to start the meal, and a dessert wine such as a rich Sauternes with the sweet if you really are lashing out.

# LAYING DOWN WINE

Pre-eminent among wines for laying down are the red wines of Bordeaux, and those fortunate enough to secure some of the 1970s, costly as they are likely to be, may expect to have treasures indeed in the late 1970s when they are ready for drinking. Consultation with a reputable wine merchant is wise.

**Storing wine at home**

In most homes storing wine does not present insuperable problems. The underground cellar, free from draught and variations of temperature is the ideal, but as few new wine drinkers today possess one, it is necessary to seek the most suitable spot in the house or flat. That may be under the stairs, under a sideboard, in an unused corner, even in or on top of a wardrobe. The site must be away from strong light, radiators, fires or hot pipes; it must also be draught-free and unlikely to be subjected to violent temperature changes. For practical purposes this sort of laying-down should be restricted to wines likely to be drunk within a year or so. For such short-term storing a room which may be 16°C

*Bottles from left to right:*
*Rhine wines—long-necked, slim and usually brown.*
*Beaujolais Pichet—club-shaped.*
*White Bordeaux—high-shouldered, clear.*
*Red Bordeaux—high-shouldered, green.*
*Moselle – as Rhine, but sometimes green.*
*Red Burgundy – sloping shoulders, green.*
*White Burgundy – sloping shoulders, usually light green.*

(60°F) in the summer and heated up to 18°C (65°F) in the winter does not threaten danger. Wines should be stored lying down to keep the cork moist (spirits should be kept standing) and a rack is the best place to store bottles without wasting space or risking damage. You may buy one to hold a dozen bottles and then build up gradually on Meccano lines. Look at the bottles occasionally and if a cork is 'weeping', drink immediately.

**What to store**

Do not store Champagne—it does not improve much in the bottle. Château-bottled Clarets and Burgundies are a good investment. Rhine wines, Sauternes and white Burgundies are also first-class wines to store. The point of the exercise is to buy wine when it is cheap enough for you to afford it, and keep it in storage until it is at its best, when it would probably be expensive to buy, though of course there is a certain gamble involved.

**When to drink the wine?**
If you read that a wine should be drunk young, like Beaujolais, that means within about three years of being bottled. If you are laying down wine, a rough guide is that Claret reaches maturity about 8–10 years after bottling, Burgundy about 5–8 years. But it depends on the particular wine and the year, so keep in touch with your supplier and check when your cellar should be ready to drink.

## WINE IN RESTAURANTS

Ideally a vintage Claret or Burgundy should be ordered well in advance with a request to decant it at the right time (the good sommelier will attach the cork to the decanter for identification). Drinking a fine wine within minutes of the cork being drawn is unfair to the establishment and certainly to the wine.

### Tasting

The pouring out by the sommelier of a sip to taste is much more than a civility: it is entirely practical, enabling the customer to judge whether or not the wine is 'corked'. This is a rare occurrence but the most delicate sniff will be enough if it is. The nose should also detect a musty smell—though this is not so unpleasant and pronounced—which can be due to a faulty stave in the cask which previously contained the wine. If there is any suggestion to your nose of vinegar, damp blankets or both, then back it must go. If you are in any doubt, invite the sommelier to 'nose' the wine too. It is part of his job to give advice, if sought, on the state of the wine or the choice of it. The trouble is, few restaurants actually have sommeliers, but the head waiter will do as well—better come armed with your own knowledge in any case.

## THE RIGHT GLASSES

The eye as well as the nose and the palate plays an essential part in the true enjoyment of wine so you must be able to see it. Size is an important consideration. The wine glass should not be too small or too big, the ideal size, I suggest, being one which holds about 4 fluid oz. (1 decilitre) when between two-thirds and three-quarters full (never fill glasses fuller than this—it will not look mean). This means that you should get rather more than six glasses out of most bottles. The Paris goblet (see page 63) is ideal for most wines, for it has a stem which can be held if the wine is white and chilled, and a plump round bowl which you may hold, if you wish, to raise the temperature of a red wine.

## DECANTING

There are very sound reasons for it, apart from the aesthetic appeal of an elegant decanter on the dinner table. It gives a good wine a chance to breathe after years in bottle and it removes any deposit which may have formed in the maturing process. Decanting is not difficult but the older the wine the more care is needed to avoid shaking up the deposit. Always wipe the neck with a clean cloth after removing seal and cork. Have a light behind the decanter so that you can see, and exclude any deposit as you pour slowly, directly or through a funnel. Most red wines will benefit from decanting a good two hours before use, and if they are very cheap and rather harsh an airing will soften and improve them. White wines can be decanted, too, though few actually benefit. These should not be served above 10°C (50°F), the reds about 16°C (60°F), average room temperature.

## RE-CORKING A BOTTLE

You may be able to put a cork back into a vin ordinaire bottle, but do not dream of doing so with a very old Claret, for example. And it is worth noting that you can buy a Champagne stopper cork which will keep any sparkling wine in good condition for several days. It has been recorded that it has kept a variety of wines drinkable for up to a week, the 'record' being several weeks. An alternative is a clean, tapered cork (from any home-made wine kit supplier).
Never put the old cork back upside down.

## DESCRIBING WINE

As for the terms met with in tasting circles, a wine is said to be hard when there is a lot of tannin in it; tannin comes from the skin of black grapes, important in lengthening the maturing period, as in Clarets, which may take twenty or more years to reach their peak. *Bouquet* (or 'nose') is the aroma—'the sweet, clean, pleasing and discreet fragrance which none but the better wines have as a gift', as it has been expressed.
'*Body*' does not necessarily suggest alcoholic strength; it refers to the amount of the various dissolved substances in the wine, including tartaric and malic acids, tannin, proteins and salts.
'*Clean*' denotes a pure wine with no unpleasant taste. A 'well-balanced' wine shows complete equilibrium among elements of aroma and taste.

### Colour, texture and taste

Many words are purely descriptive of colour, texture and taste. Though it takes an expert to separate the constitu-

ents and to assess what a very hard young wine may be like in ten or even twenty years' time, amateurs can get a lot out of tasting. Often enough the tasting notes of connoisseurs are far from frighteningly technical and could well be equalled by the earnest student. For instance, smooth or velvety are words often used to denote good texture, harsh and rough, bad texture. And simple, rustic, comparisons in bouquet and taste are often made with, for example, raspberries, hazelnuts, violets, peaches and blackcurrants.

## READING THE LABELS

Labels tend to be more informative —and more honest—than some of them once were. More stringent laws in the wine-producing areas, and insistence of some countries (like Britain) on displaying the country of origin have helped to bring a new respectability even to the cheapest wines. Names of well-known producers give evidence of quality, too— Calvet or Cordier on a Bordeaux bottle, Langenbach or Deinhard on Moselle and Hock bottles, for example.

### French Labels

There are four types of label for Bordeaux wines:
1 Label for château-bottled wine will carry the words 'Mise en bouteilles'.
2 Label for wine bottled by the shipper will carry the name of the wine and the

words 'bottled by . . .' (the label will be to the shipper's own design).

3  Label for *Monopole* or registered private brand—the shipper's own blend of various wines from a particular region, on which his reputation for discrimination and honesty is based.

4  District or commune label. It is easy at first to confuse this with the château-bottled label. A label saying, for example 'St. Julien' means 'the wine in this bottle bottle came from the St. Julien district' and the wine will not necessarily come from one vineyard, but be a blend from several made by the shipper and the quality will depend entirely on the shipper. Once again, find out from your wine shop who the most reliable shippers are. Burgundy labels follow a different pattern. They give the name of the vineyard if it is famous, the name of the district if that is more famous, and if neither is well-known, the wine will simply be described as 'Côte de Nuits' or 'Côte de Beaune'.

### German Labels

There are four types corresponding to the Bordeaux system, except that the word 'Estate' is used instead of '*Château*'. German labels must also give vintage date, name of district where the grapes (or at least 50% of them) were grown, and the name of the shipper. They may also carry the words 'Fuder No. . . .' meaning the number of the cask from which the wine was taken.

# TERMINOLOGY

### French Terms

*\*Appellation contrôlée:* conforms to French Government's requirements as to quality, area of origin and specific grapes used.

*Brut:* Unsweetened, as applied to very dry Champagne or other sparkling wines (See also *Extra Sec*).

*Chambrer:* To bring wine to room temperature.

*Climat:* Vineyard.

*Clos:* Enclosure (particularly the once walled in vineyards of Burgundy).

*Cru:* Growth—the wine from a single vineyard. *Premier cru:* First growth—the finest wine of its type (see Claret, Red Bordeaux).

*Cru bourgeois:* Attractive and reasonably-priced wines from unclassified single Bordeaux vineyards.

*Cuvée:* From one vat. *Première cuvée:* first and best pressing of the grapes.

*Domaine:* Property (used in Burgundy; *château* used in Bordeaux).

*Doux:* Soft, sweet—particularly a sweet Champagne.

*Extra Sec:* Dry, but less dry than *Brut*. (See also *Sec*, *Demi-sec*).

*Grande marque:* Traditional term

*Lunch time in Italy, with white wine.*

indicating top-quality Champagne (Champagnes are known by the names of the Houses producing them).

*Méthode champenoise:* Sparkling produced by the Champagne method.

*\*Mise en bouteille au château:* Wine bottled by château-owner (name of château and, usually, vintage date will be stamped on cork).

*Mousseux:* Sparkling.

*Nature:* Wine to which no sugar has been added.

*Pétillant:* Slightly sparkling.

*Sec:* Medium dry (*Demi-sec:* Rather sweet).

*Sommelier:* A waiter who advises on and serves wines and spirits (usually wears a badge of a bunch of grapes).

*Vendange:* Vintage—a vintage wine bearing a year was made from grapes gathered in that year.

*Non-vintage* (or *NV*) is a blend of wines made in different years which were of consistent quality.

*\*VDQS:* Indicates a wine recognized to be of superior quality. One grade lower than *Appellation contrôlée*. (*Vin délimité de qualité supérieur*.)

*Vin ordinaire:* Ordinary, cheap wine for everyday drinking.

### German Terms

These tend to be of unwieldy length, but

there are certain words which will help the buyer to choose (*Estate bottled* means what it says—the same thing as *château-bottled* in the French terms):

*Abfüllung:* Bottled by.

*Auslese:* High-class wine from specially-selected mature grapes.

*Beerenauslese:* Rare, high-class wine from grapes picked almost individually, after they have been left on the vines until they are like raisins and their sugar concentration is at its highest.

*Feine, Feinste, Hochfein:* Fine/finest.

*Kabinett:* High-class wine.

*Kellar-Abzug:* Cellar-bottled (by wine merchant).

*\*Originalabfüllung:* Bottled by grower at place of production.

*Quälitatswein mit Prädikät:* Wine of highest class. *Qualitätswein:* Wine from a defined region and of tested quality.

*Tafelwein:* Light home-grown wine of minimum alcoholic strength.

*Schloss-Abzug:* Castle-bottled (by wine merchant).

*Sekt:* Sparkling.

*Spätlese:* Wine made from grapes picked late in mature condition.

*Spritzig:* Slightly sparkling.

*Weinberg:* Vineyard.

### Italian Terms

*Abboccato:* Sweet white wine.

*Bianco:* (in Spanish *Blanco*): White.

*Rosso:* (in Spanish *Tinto*): Red.

*Dolce* (in Spanish *Dulce*): Sweet.

*Frizzante:* Semi-sparkling.

*Rosato* (in Spanish *Rosado*): Pink (Rosé).

*Secco* (in Spanish *Seco*): Dry.

*Spumante:* Sparkling.

### English Terms

*Bouquet* (or *Nose*): Aroma.

*Body:* The dissolved particles in the wine, giving it its full, rounded taste.

*Clean:* A pure wine with no unpleasant taste.

*Dry:* Unsweetened.

*Must:* Unfermented grape juice, immediately after pressing.

*Vintage/Non-vintage:* See French terms.

*Reserve/Special reserve:* High-quality wines specially set aside by the estate for this description—means, roughly, the best of the best.

*Well-balanced:* A wine with good equilibrium between aroma and taste.

*Note:* The terms marked * are well worth memorizing. *Appellation contrôlée* and *VDQS* will ensure a good, reasonably priced wine. *Mise en bouteille* (or *Mise du Château*) and *Originalabfüllung* will guarantee a wine of superlative quality at impressive cost. Italy has yet to come up with anything comparable in these categories, but the name 'Chianti' is strictly controlled, so any wine bearing the name is usually of consistently good quality.

# WHERE WINE COMES FROM NORTH, SOUTH, EAST, WEST

*The world's vineyard acreage today is greater than ever it has been since the first vines flourished. The top map gives some of the major wine-producing areas of Europe, the other shows where wine comes from around the globe.*

There is some evidence that wine-making was practised in Mesozoic times, perhaps ten or even twelve thousand years ago. Earlier than 5000 BC wine was being made and drunk in Egypt and Mesopotamia. And part of the decor of the tomb of Phtah-Hotep, who died about 4000 BC shows the harvesting and pressing of grapes. France is one of the oldest of all wine-growing areas. Fossils found at Cezanne, in the Marne Valley, have upon them impressions of wild vines. And when the Phoenicians started to build Marseilles in 600 BC there were vines already flourishing. France today has some four million acres of vineyards and it is true to say that her products set the standards by which all the world's wines are liable to be judged. Climate and soil play a vital part—from Burgundy's clay and gravel; the stony granite dust and sun-reflecting red-brown boulders of the Rhône Valley; the gravel and sand of the Bordeaux region; the gentle, right-way-facing slopes of the Champagne area; and from the verdant Loire.

Italy, the biggest wine producer, has vineyards scattered from the great growing area among the lakes in the North to below Naples, with Piedmont perhaps the most illustrious region and source of Barolo, the finest of all Italian red wines, as Julius Caesar decided. Austria's best wines, mostly white, come from the neighbourhood of Krems and of Durnstein, and the best Swiss wines are grown upon the banks of Lakes Neuchatel and Geneva.

Spain produces a great quantity of table wines, but the best are the wines of the Rioja (both red and white). Much wine comes, too, from Valdepeñas in the Don Quixote province of La Mancha—wines of high alcoholic strength—and also from Tarragona and Alicante. Portugal produces, from the Minho province in the North, the dry, slightly spritzig and refreshing Vinhos Verdes, full-bodied Burgundian-style reds from the slopes above the Dão and Mondego Rivers, and a dessert wine of some merit from Setubal, south of Lisbon.

Germany's wine production is relatively small but some of the greatest of all white wines come from the grapes, chiefly Riesling, grown on the steep, often almost sheer slate and flinty slopes above the Rivers Rhine, Moselle, Nahe, Neckar, Main, Saar and Ruwer. Yugoslavia's white wines from the Riesling, Sylvaner and Traminer grapes mostly emanate from Slovenia, near the Austrian border, with Lutomer Riesling from the north, far the best known abroad, though there are Macedonian wines equally good. Palatable reds come from Central Europe (also whites), the Balkans, North Africa and South America.

Australia produces a wide variety of attractive and sound wines, mainly from New South Wales, where vines were planted in the 18th century, and South Australia, now by far the biggest producing area—especially the Barossa Valley—and also in Western Australia, Victoria and Queensland.

South Africa's wine industry is a good deal older; first vines were planted in the Cape in 1655. Paarl and Stellenbosch yield some of the best white wines.

Canada's wine production is small and mainly restricted to Ontario and British Columbia. But the United States makes very considerable quantities of wine of many types, mainly in California but also in Upper New York State, Ohio and Pennsylvania. Many grape varieties were imported from Europe in the last century.

Lastly, England is a minor wine producer commercially, mainly at Horam, Sussex and Hambledon, Hampshire.

Rioja

**SPAIN**

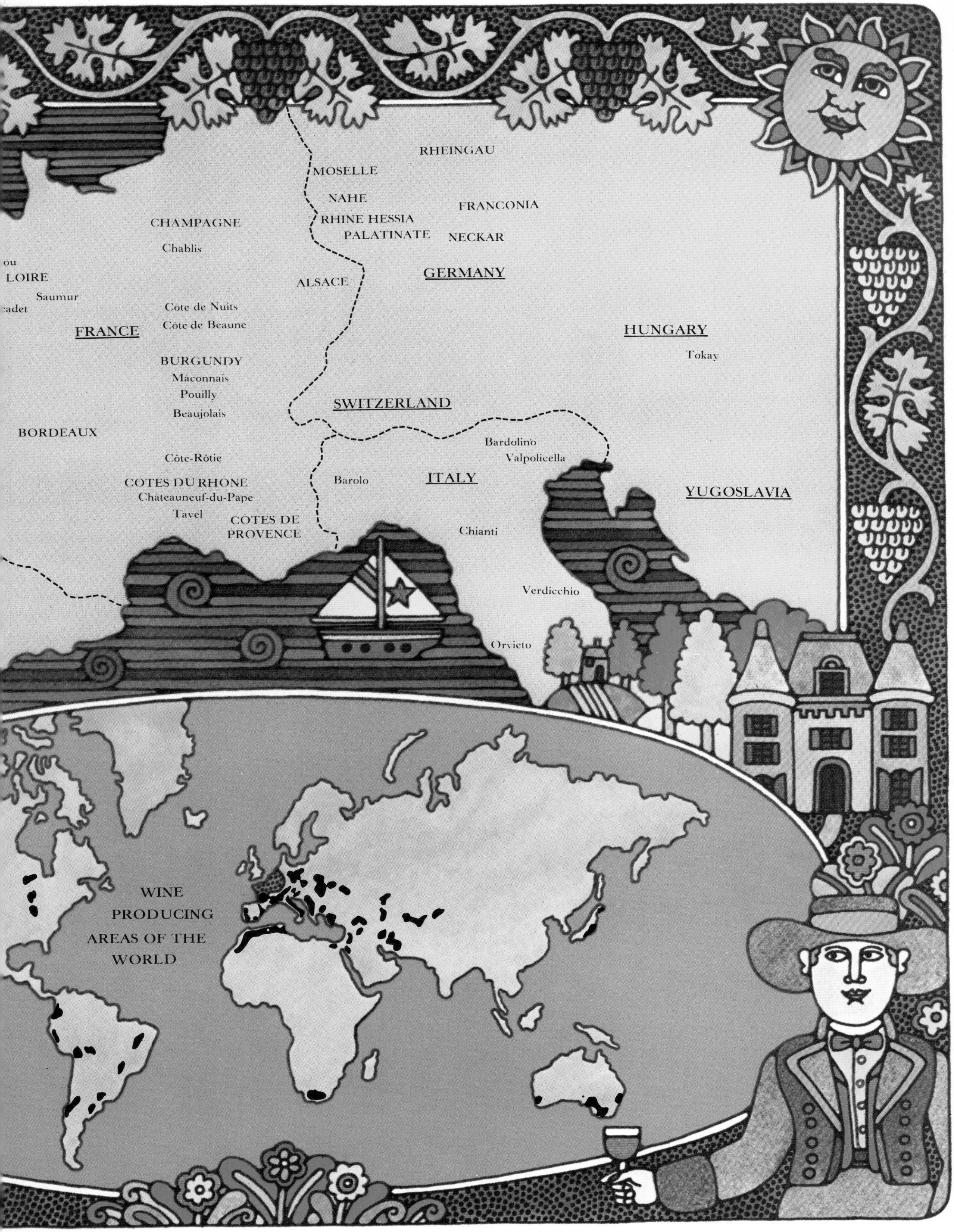

RHEINGAU

MOSELLE

NAHE

FRANCONIA

RHINE HESSIA

PALATINATE    NECKAR

CHAMPAGNE

Chablis

LOIRE

Saumur

cadet

GERMANY

ALSACE

Côte de Nuits

FRANCE

Côte de Beaune

HUNGARY

Tokay

BURGUNDY

Mâconnais

Pouilly

Beaujolais

SWITZERLAND

BORDEAUX

Bardolino

Côte-Rôtie

Valpolicella

COTES DU RHONE

Barolo

ITALY

YUGOSLAVIA

Châteauneuf-du-Pape

Tavel

COTES DE

Chianti

PROVENCE

Verdicchio

Orvieto

WINE

PRODUCING

AREAS OF THE

WORLD

25

# RED BORDEAUX

*The red wines of Bordeaux are commonly known as Claret in English, and include some of the noblest and most subtle wines in the world.*

## CLARET (RED BORDEAUX)

The table is divided into the main areas of Bordeaux which produce Claret (Haut Médoc is further divided into its most famous *communes*); then follow the names of a few of the wines produced within the area.

### Haut Médoc
ST. ESTEPHE
*Château Beau-Site, Château de Pez, Château Calon Ségur, Château Montrose*
ST.-JULIEN
*Château Beychevelle, Château Léoville Barton, Château Talbot*
CANTENAC
*Château Palmer, Château d'Issan*
PAUILLAC
*Château Lafite-Rothschild\*, Château Latour\*, Château Mouton-Rothschild\**
MARGAUX
*Château Margaux, Château Rauzan Gassies, Château Rausan Segla*

### St.-Emilion
*Château Cheval Blanc\*, Château Ausone, Château Canon, Château Figeac, Château Clos Fourtet*

### Pomerol
*Château Petrus\*, Château La Conseillante, Château l'Evangile, Vieux Château Certan*

### Graves
*Château Haut-Brion\*, Château Carbonnieux, Domaine de Chevalier, Château La Mission Haut-Brion, Château Smith-Haut-Lafitte*

### Fronsac, Blaye, Bourge
*Communes producing robust red wines of medium quality*

### Premières Côtes de Bordeaux
*The area produces some red wine of reasonable quality, but far more white wine (see page 30)*

\* = very fine and very costly

For three centuries following 1152, when Eleanor of Aquitaine married Henry II of England, considerable areas of France were under English rule, and they included the Bordeaux wine area. The British drank more of the wine *per capita* at that time than they do today. At one stage, 300 ships were engaged in the trade, and wine accounted for almost a third of all British imports.

Now, there is a growing world demand for the finest of the Bordeaux wines, especially from America and, to an increasing extent, Japan, and this means, of course, that they are becoming scarcer and more expensive.

In a very general way, one can say that the wines of Bordeaux are more delicate than those of Burgundy, and that the most noble Clarets have a subtlety and finesse unmatched by any other red wine in the world. Even so, the red wines of Bordeaux and Burgundy have an affinity, especially those of St.-Emilion with those from north-west of Beaune. Certainly among the less exalted wines from both areas, one can easily be mistaken for another.

In general again, Bordeaux wines take longer to mature: Clarets are drinkable after about three years, but reach their best after some ten to fifteen years, depending on the vintage. Some of the finest continue to improve for thirty years or more, though whether such a leisurely process will go on being possible, now that world demand is increasing, is questionable.

The Bordeaux wine area produces a huge quantity of high-quality wines—ten times that of Burgundy. Its 300,000 or so acres of vineyards are all contained within the Department of the Gironde. The whole area is divided into districts, each having a different soil structure, which helps to account for the wide range of the types and styles of wine. These in turn are divided into communes or parishes, in which the estates are situated. The largest of these are known as Châteaux, Domaines, or sometimes Clos, and the best wines are known by the names of the properties on which they are produced.

The Médoc (from the Bas Médoc in the north, near to Bordeaux itself, to the Haut Médoc in the south, at the mouth of the River Gironde) is the supreme Claret area, and has more than 500 châteaux, ranging from great and historic estates to small-holdings of a tiny area. The chief Médoc communes, so distinguished in the world's wine-lists, are St.-Estèphe, St.-Julien, Pauillac, Cantenac and Margaux.

The Classification of 1855, suggested by Napoleon III for the Paris Exhibition, was originally intended only for wines from the Médoc, and three of them—Château Latour and Château Lafite-Rothschild from Pauillac, and Château-Margaux from the commune of Margaux—were given Premier Cru rating. They were joined in their distinction by an 'odd man out'—Château Haut-Brion from Graves. Château Mouton-Rothschild, although classified as a 'second growth' is, even so, one of the greatest Clarets, and costs as much as the wines of the first growth.

The Clarets of the Médoc are, broadly, dry, but whereas those of Pauillac and St.-Estèphe are full-flavoured, those of St.-Julien, Margaux and Cantenac are lighter. A St.-Emilion Claret is fuller-bodied than a Médoc, a Pomerol wine is lighter, soft, with a distinctive bouquet, and from Graves the Clarets are fine and dry. (Clarets generally have an alcoholic content of 10° to 11°.)

Wines classified as lesser growths have not risen so spectacularly in price as the great aristocrats: a 1961 Château Beau-Site from St.-Estephe is ready for drinking now, and a 1970 Château de Pez, also from St.-Estèphe, and full of promise, is for laying down, and neither of these wines is at all exorbitant in price. Like the wines they produce, the châteaux themselves are not all grand or beautiful. But some, like the Château Lafite-Rothschild, belonging to the Barons de Rothschild, *are* magnificent. The Château Beychevelle (whose wine is classified as fourth growth) is one of the loveliest in St.-Julien, as serene and symmetrical as the elegant Château Talbot, which was built on the site of the castle belonging to the last English defender of Bordeaux, who was killed at Castillon in 1453.

These châteaux all have famous names, but the lesser growths, the non-vintage commune wines, the strong 'Bordeaux Supérieures Rouges' from the Médoc, and the humbler but sturdy favourites like Appellation Médoc, Appellation St.-Emilion and simply 'Bordeaux Rouge' can embellish many dishes, particularly roast meat and poultry. They can also still all be found at a really low price.

### Recent Good Vintages
1962, 1964, 1966, 1967, 1970

*Top left: grapes being picked at the Château Loudenne at St. Yzans-de-Médoc.*
*Below: cellarman at Leith's restaurant carefully laying down his Clarets.*
*Right: Claret glass and decanter.*

26

# RED BURGUNDY

*Most Burgundy wines are dry and tend to be more robust, and sometimes heavier, than the red wines of Bordeaux.*

## BURGUNDY

The table is divided into the main regions of the Burgundy area; the names of districts *(communes)* within a region are in capital letters (these names always appear on labels), and then follow the names of a few of the vineyards in each district.

### Côte de Nuits (northern part of Côte d'Or)
**GEVREY-CHAMBERTIN**
*Chambertin, Clos de Bèze\*, Clos St. Jacques, Charmes, Griotte, Latricières*
**CHAMBOLLE-MUSIGNY**
*Amoureuses, Le Musigny\*, Bonnes Mares, Vieilles Vignes*
**VOUGEOT**
*Clos de Vougeot*
**VOSNE-ROMANEE**
*Romanée-Conti\*, Romanée St. Vivant, La Tache\*, La Romanée\*, Le Richebourg\*, Malconsorts, Grands-Echezeaux\**
**MOREY ST.-DENIS**
*Clos des Lambrays, Clos de la Roche, Clos de Tart*
**NUITS-ST.-GEORGES**
*Boudots, Cailles, Clos de la Maréchale, Porrets, Pruliers, Vaucrains, St.-Georges*

### Côte de Beaune (southern part of Côte d'Or)
**ALOXE-CORTON**
*Bressandes, Le Corton, Renardes, Clos du Roi*
**VOLNAY**
*Caillerets, Champans, Santenots*
**POMMARD**
*Chanlins, Épenots, La Platière, Pezerolles, Rugiens*
**SANTENAY**
*Les Gravières*
**BEAUNE**
*Avaux, Boucherottes, Champs-Pimont, Grèves, Clos des Mouches, Theurons*

### Hospices de Beaune
*The Hospices own various vineyards in the Côte de Beaune. Wines are sold as Hospices, plus the names of old benefactors. Of good quality and expensive*

### Côte Chalonnaise
*Mercurey*

### Beaujolais
*The names below are those of districts:*

St. Amour, Brouilly, Juliénas, Morgon, Fleurie, Moulin-à-Vent

### Mâcon
*No distinguished red wines, but acceptable for everyday drinking*

---

\* = very fine and very costly

The vineyards of Burgundy stretch from Auxerre almost to Lyon in France, and have existed for more than a thousand years. In the twelfth century wines made by monks found favour at the court of the Dukes of Burgundy, and much later, when Louis XIV drank the wines of the Côte d'Or on his doctor's advice, his patronage ensured their fame, based on the maintenance of high standards. (Incidentally, 'Burgundy' is an anglicized version of Bourgogne).

The Côte de Nuits, the northern part of the Côte d'Or, produces very little white wine, but is world-famous for its red wines, full-bodied, with a magnificent bouquet, and maturing more slowly than the red wines of the Côte de Beaune, in the south of the Côte d'Or.

One of the finest, La Romanée-Conti, is rare now in Britain, because of competition from America. But there is justice in this: La Romanée-Conti was one of the last vineyards with old root stock saved from a *phylloxera* attack; however, after the last war, these old vines had to go, and the vineyard was planted with French Pinot Noir grapes (used for the making of good red wines in both the Côte de Nuits and the Côte de Beaune), grafted onto *phylloxera*-resistant American briars.

Chambertin is another wine which has always been famous in Britain and is now much sought after in America, Canada and many other countries. It comes from two vineyards in the Gevrey-Chambertin *commune*, Chambertin and Chambertin Clos de Bèze, divided between twenty-five owners. This accounts for the fact that even Chambertins of the same vintage can vary considerably. At its best, though, Chambertin is one of the leading six Burgundies, combining grace with vigour, firmness with finesse, and exuding a glorious bouquet. Its alcoholic strength is 11.5°.

The Côte de Beaune, famous for its white wines (see page 32) produces red wines lighter in style than those of the Côte de Nuits. At Beaune, the main centre is the Hospices de Beaune, the owner of thirty-one vineyards left to it by wealthy benefactors. The wine is usually auctioned on the third Sunday in November, and the bidding is done 'by the candle': three small candles are lit as a lot is put up for sale, and the last bid received before the third candle goes out is the successful one.

Hospices wines are sold by the name of the donor, and this appears on the label. One of the most famous is Hospices de Beaune, Beaune, Cuvée Guigone de Salins—and Guigone de Salins founded the Hospices in 1443.

Red Burgundies are generally more robust and assertive, less complex and therefore easier to appreciate than Clarets. Beaujolais especially matures much more quickly—so fast, in fact, that it is drunk within a year of the vintage—and even, as 'Beaujolais nouveau', within weeks of bottling. The Gamay grape, which normally results in an acid wine, produces in the Beaujolais district a wine that is light, fruity and fresh. It can range in quality from an undemanding, drinkable blend without any handle to its name, to something more exalted: 'Beaujolais Supérieur', for example, comes from a restricted area (though a fairly wide one); 'Beaujolais Villages' comes from a more narrowly defined production area, and then there are wines entitled to bear the name of their *cru*, like St. Amour, Brouilly, Juliénas, Fleurie, Moulin-à-Vent and Morgon. Beaujolais is the southernmost area of the Burgundy region. The Côte Mâconnais, which adjoins it, is famous for its white Burgundy; its red wines are as good as any *vin de table* for everyday drinking. This is true, too, of the plain Beaujolais. Beaujolais wines generally are cheaper than most Burgundies, although the '*crus*' are rather more expensive than the others from the region. Burgundy should generally be served at room temperature, but Beaujolais wines should be drunk cool.

---

### Main Types of Grape
Pinot Noir: *used for the fine red wines of the Côte de Nuits and the Côte de Beaune.*
Gamay: *used for the light, fresh fruity wines of Beaujolais.*

---

### Recent Good Vintages
1961, 1964, 1966, 1969

---

*A fine, robust, well-rounded red Burgundy is excellent with game, steak and rich patés.*

# RED WINES OF THE WORLD

*Apart from France, the main red wine exporting countries are Italy, Spain, Portugal and South Africa. Of these, probably Italy produces the most varied range—from Piedmont in the mountainous north, to Calabria in the south. But the United States and Australia are turning into major wine growing areas too.*

Although none competes with the great wines of Burgundy and Bordeaux, there are vintage Italian wines, and Spanish wines too, of considerable merit. They could very well find their way into many more lists, now that the prices of the classic reds of France are soaring so high.

## ITALY

The rise in imports of Italian wines into Britain, for example, during 1972, was unprecedented—the fastest growth rate of any European wine-supplying country. And most significant was the increased quantity of quality wines: something like three-quarters of the total were bottled in Italy. She is the largest wine producer in the world, with an annual output of about 1,540 million gallons, of which 187 million gallons are exported, mainly to Common Market countries, the United States and Britain. Considerable quantities now carry the D.O.C. (Denominazione di Origine Controllata) seal, similar to France's Appellation Contrôlée, and this is not lightly bestowed. It has been in force since 1963, but growers in some areas had their own consortia laws, like those of Chianti Classico, for example, which go back to 1932.

Italian wine names are indicative of the grape used—Barbera, Vernaccia, Lagrein; alternatively, they may take the name of a place which is also a district (Chianti, Valpolicella, Etna, for example), or of a district to which a single place has given its name, like Barolo, Barbaresco, Orvieto. Barolo from Piedmont, one of Italy's larger wine regions, I have for a long time regarded as the best of all Italian wines. It is made from the Nebbiolo grape, and although comparisons are rarely quite fair, as an indication of its robust nature and characteristics I would say that it is nearer to the best Rhônes than to any other reds. It has been described as 'dry and smooth, velvety and full-bodied' and having 'a superb perfume of violets against a tarry background'. Barolo is aged in wood for three years and goes on maturing in bottle: a 1962 which I drank ten years later had a lot of depth and a hint of hardness, which suggested that it would go on improving for quite a time. Similar, but quicker to mature, are Barbaresco (a town with a red Roman tower) and Barbera, which is fruity and usually drunk young.

Verona's three wines are all named after places nearby—Valpolicella and Bardolino (both reds) and a white, Soave. Bardolino, from the shore of Lake Garda, has a distinctive charm and, like Valpolicella, is generally lighter than the wines of Piedmont or Tuscany, the home of Chianti. This varies widely, from the light and fresh (to be drunk young), to the more austere, darker 'Chianti Classico' wines which will improve considerably with age. Less well known are the wines of Torgiano, just south of Perugia, which also age gracefully (I found a 1964 delightful). They have a most attractive deep ruby colour, a fragrant 'nose', dryness and good balance.

### Some Italian red wines

Barolo: *good bouquet, full-bodied, needs time to mature*
Valpolicella: *fruity, soft and full*
Barbera: *fruity and powerful*
Chianti (Classico): *austere, needs time to mature*
Sangiovese: *full*
Barbaresco: *a little lighter than Barolo*
Bardolino: *lighter than Barolo*
Grignolino: *light*
Valtenesi: *light*
Frosinone: *both dry and sweet*
Brachetto: *sparkling, semi-sweet*
Lambrusco: *sparkling, dry*
Barbacarlo: *often frizzante*
Buttafuoco: *often frizzante*

## SPAIN

The red wines of Spain have suffered, rather unfairly, from their 'image' as the cheapest in the supermarkets and (by the glass) in bars. Certainly a vast gallonage is now brought by tanker to be bottled under supermarket names, or brand names like 'Rocamar', 'La Vista' or 'Don Cortez', and these are admirable within their price range. But, from the Rioja district especially, there are some splendid reds of character and age, like Fuenmayor A.G.E. Consecha 1954, which is bottled in Spain. 'Consecha' means vintage, but not necessarily in the sense of 'all of one year'. By local custom, some excellent wines keep the original date although they have been 'refreshed' with later good vintages, on the same principle as the Solera system for making Sherry.

About these wines, however, there is consistency as well as maturity. From Haro, in the Rioja, are shipped some admirable 'consecha' wines which are liable to become better known. One of them is a red with plenty of body and fruitiness, labelled simply Gran Reserva. Both the 1955 and the 1957 I found to have character if not great distinction, and to represent good value in the context of today's prices. This may be said, too, of the cheaper, more flowery Vina Vial (described as Burgundy-type), and the light red Banda Azul.

## PORTUGAL

Portugal's red table wines are, perhaps, less ranging, with few vintage wines. Here again, we have become accustomed to brand names like 'Justina'. Two Portuguese reds which are unpretentious but usually good value are Periquita, big and full-bodied, and Vila Real, lighter in colour as well as in body, and nearer in style to Claret than to Burgundy. Full-bodied and Burgundian in style are the Dão wines—the familiar brand names are 'Alianca' and 'Gran Vaoco'. They come from the terraced hillsides rising from the Dão and Mondego Rivers, and they age well; I have drunk a 1962 of character and distinction.

Portugal produces a few other noteworthy red wines with connections of historical interest to British people: for example, from the district close to the baroque palaces of Cintra (where Byron wrote 'Childe Harold') comes a red beverage wine, Colares, somewhat similar to a Rhône and a good deal less powerful than the red from Torres, a place made famous by Wellington in the Peninsular War.

## SWITZERLAND

Swiss wines often have a light sparkle and can be drunk young. They are not exported in quantity because of their comparatively high cost, but two are well known—Dôle and Cortaillod—both fresh, light and fruity.

## ARGENTINA

Argentina is one of the largest wine-producing countries in the world, and not very much of it is exported—

perhaps because the Argentinians drink
it all themselves! The reds are sound and
some of the best are sold under the labels
of Cabernet Reservado and Cavrodilla
Tinto.

## CHILE
The Chilean red wine Cabernet, named
after the grape, is darkish and smooth,
and is popular in North America as well
as Britain.

## RUSSIA
The Mukuzani red from Georgia is
worth a trial.

## MOROCCO
Moroccan reds can be economical as
well as agreeable for everyday drinking;
one I commend is Sidi Mabrouck.

## ISRAEL
Apart from a 'Claret', these are inclined
to be sweetish.

## HUNGARY
The best known abroad is Bull's Blood,
from Eger, a robust, heavy, dark red
wine. It is as strong as a Rhône, and as
soft as a Burgundy and matures for
several years in wooden barrels, placed
in rock caves.

## UNITED STATES
The United States is seventh in the
world list of wine-producing countries
and its vineyards are based on stocks
from Burgundy, Bordeaux, Alsace and
the Rhine. Most US labels carry the
names of these original stocks, and many
European types of wine are emulated—
Burgundy, Claret, and so on. Many of
the best wines come from north of San
Francisco, and most of these Californian
wines are blended, though there are a
few estate-bottled wines, some very
good ones amongst them.

## AUSTRALIA
Australia exports some splendid reds,
that deserve greater favour. Many of
them have the French 'Burgundy' or
'Claret' descriptions, but Australians
claim that their best wines are delicious
in their own right, and should not be
compared with European ones.
The main area for red table wines
stretches between Adelaide and Sydney
(where the first vines were planted in
1788), and includes the Hunter and
Barossa Valleys, the area north-west of
Brisbane, the Roma district and the
Swan Valley, close to Perth.
Two Australian wines particularly to be
commended are Wynn's Coonawarra
Estate Cabernet and Tahbilk Estate
Shiraz.

## SOUTH AFRICA
Some dependable reds—like the fruity
Nederberg Cabernet.

*A wine rack stacked with red wines from
all over the world, and a bottle of
Chianti in its typical straw 'fiasco'.*

# WHITE BORDEAUX AND BURGUNDY

*From Bordeaux comes the legendary (and extremely costly!) Château d'Yquem, while Burgundy is the home of Chablis.*

## WHITE BORDEAUX
from the districts of:

**Graves** (dry and sweet wines)
*Leading châteaux: Carbonnieux, Girafe, Laville Haut-Brion\*, Olivier*

**Sauternes** (producing sweet wines)
Comprise the communes of:
Sauternes, Barsac, Bommes, Fargues and Preignac
*Leading châteaux: Yquem\*, Climens, Coutet, Doisy-Daëne, Filhot, Lafaurie-Peyraguey, La Tour Blanche*

**Entre-Deux-Mers** (producing medium quality dry wines)

**Cerons** (wines between Graves and Sauternes for sweetness)

**Premières Côtes de Bordeaux** (producing medium sweet wine)

\* = very fine and very costly

Graves whites are of two kinds—dry and sweet. The dry wines are considered to be less dry and clean than—say—a good Chablis, but are, even so, light and agreeable. The most distinguished of them is the Château Laville Haut-Brion, very dry and clean with a hint of honey on the 'nose'; the most popular (and rather less costly) are Château Olivier and Château Carbonnieux.
Entre-Deux-Mers is the largest wine-producing area of the Gironde Department, covering the land between the Garonne and Dordogne Rivers until they meet to become the Gironde. Wines bearing its name used to be sweet, but since the growers were prevented from sweetening them, they are dry and light, and a favourite accompaniment locally to Arcachon oysters and other sea-food from the Gulf of Gascony. Entre-Deux-Rives is the name of one sweet wine now on the market in Britain—really a more accurate one. The wines of this area are entitled to 'Appellation Contrôlée Bordeaux Supérieur' when their alcoholic strength is not less than 11·5%. The golden colour and the richness of the best of the Sauternes is not matched by a sweet Graves. Château Yquem (or d'Yquem), Grand Premier Cru classé Sauternes, is the aristocrat among aristocrats in the realm of extremely costly dessert wines. It is an opulent old-gold colour and has intense, mouth-filling flavour and a rich, heady perfume. The grapes, grown in one of the most perfectly maintained vineyards in the world (it can only be visited by appointment), are picked almost individually at the precise stage known as *la pourriture noble* ('the noble rot')—a fungus called *Botrytis cinerea*, to make Yquem the full, long-living, lusciously sweet Queen of Sauternes. It should be served cool but never iced, and only with fruit or fruit dishes, or as a dessert alternative to Port. Quantities should be small—which is fortunate, since Yquem is extremely costly.
Another Sauternes, a rich dessert wine of real distinction, is Château Climens.

### Recent Good Vintages
1961, 1962, 1969, 1970

## WHITE BURGUNDY
from the districts of:

**Chablis**
Wine from this area is divided into four categories:
(1) Grand cru (the best of all) produced by the following vineyards
*Vaudésir, Les Preuses, Les Clos, Grenouille, Valmur, Blanchotte, Bourgos*
(2) Premier cru
(3) Chablis
(4) Petit Chablis (best drunk young)

**Côte de Nuits**
VOUGEOT
*Clos Blan de Vougeot, Côte de Beaune*
ALOXE-CORTON
*Corton-Charlemagne*
MEURSAULT
*Les Perrières, Charmes*
MONTRACHET
*Le Montrachet\*, Bâtard Montrachet,*

**Cote Chalonnaise**
*Rully-Raclot*

**Cote Mâconnaise (Mâcon)**
*Pouilly Fuissé   Mâcon Blanc*

**Beaujolais**
Beaujolais Blanc is very similar to Mâcon Blanc

\* = very fine and very costly

Burgundy produces a considerable number of white wines mainly from two regions—Chablis and the Côte de Beaune. The list above gives the names of a few of the many fine wines.
The Chablis wines are dry and the better ones are a very delicate pale gold colour, with a greenish tint and a hint of flint in the flavour. Demand for the best is great, so they are in very short supply. But beware: if a bottle is simply labelled Chablis, with no named vineyard, it may simply be acid.
Meursault is the centre for the white wines of the Côte de Beaune, and produces some of the best of all itself. The Appellation may be followed by 'Premier cru' or the name of a *climat* (vineyard), and one of the finest of these is Les Perrières, which produces a delicate, fragrant and delicious white wine. The best Meursaults are steely-dry (and yet mellow, too, oddly enough), full and high in alcohol (11·5%); their colour is a greenish gold and they have a hint of hazelnuts on the palate.
Other great white Burgundies are the firm and flowery Corton-Charlemagne from Aloxe-Corton (the Emperor Charlemagne once owned the vineyards), and Montrachet, which some wine-lovers call the finest white wine in the world, finer even than Château Yquem and the great Hocks. A Montrachet 1969, Domaine bottled, may cost as much as six times the price of a Puligny Montrachet Premier Cru, or a Chassagne Montrachet, both of the same year. (The Montrachet vineyards, by the way, lie across the borders of the two villages of Puligny and Chassagne, and either of them may give their name to the aristocrat.)
There are, happily, many reasonable if unpretentious Burgundies to be bought at reasonable prices. Pouilly Fuissé from the Côte Mâconnaise is a notable one, pale gold, dry and delicate. And there are, too, the fresh, dry wines called simply Beaujolais Blanc (which should be drunk young) and Mâcon Blanc.

### Recent good vintages
1961, 1962, 1967, 1969, 1970

*Above: a typical château on the Circuit du Sauternais, close to the Château d'Yquem. Below: scenes in the Cote de Beaune area.*

# RHÔNE, LOIRE AND ALSACE

*The wines of the Rhône, the Loire and Alsace have considerable merit and are deservedly popular in many parts of the world.*

## COTES DU RHONE WINES

Principle wines of this district are:
*Red: Châteauneuf-du-Pape, Cornas, Côte Rôtie, St.-Joseph.*
*Red and white: Crozes-Hermitage, Hermitage.*
*White: Condrieu, St.-Péray.*
*White and rosé: Lirac.*
*Rosé: Tavel*

The Rhône links the sun-warmed Mediterranean with the snowy Alps, and was the route chosen by Hannibal to take his elephants from Spain into Italy. Since Roman days, the steep, stony slopes of the Rhône Valley have been planted with vines yielding wine of a most generous nature. The two main characteristics of the Rhône wine are stability and keeping quality.

For someone taking Hannibal's journey in reverse, the starting-point for their pilgrimage of 125 miles down the narrow valley between Lyon and Avignon is the Côte Rotie, most northern point in the Côtes du Rhône. Here are the two hills called Côte Brune and Côte Blonde (the latter has this name because of the large amount of lime in the soil), and they yield the finest and most elegant red wines of the Côtes du Rhône, those of Brune being, in fact, slightly superior. Côte Rôtie wine is lighter than the widely-renowned Châteauneuf-du-Pape and, considering its quality, surprisingly inexpensive, though blended Côtes du Rhône wines are cheaper, of course. South of the Côte Rôtie is Condrieu, where some fine white wines are made, golden in colour and not less than 11% in alcoholic strength. They are, unhappily, small in quantity and so, to savour a superb Château Grillet it is necessary to go to the region—a wine safari much to be recommended!

Southwards, again, is the Hermitage Hill, rising a thousand feet above the tranquil town of Tain l'Hermitage. On the slopes of the Hill there are a great quantity of vines. The black Syrah grape predominates, and the proportion of red wines to white is about two-thirds. Both red and white display breeding, with a hint of honeysuckle on the nose; the white wines are big and dry. Both red and white are not at their best until they are six or more years old.

Châteauneuf-du-Pape comes from vineyards stretching across what is believed to be an extinct volcano. A wide variety of vines produce the powerful reds and whites (the rosés are dealt with on page 41), both made from thirteen or fourteen different grapes. Their minimum alcoholic strength is 12.5% and often more—14% or so. This accounts for them being called 'gutsy' wines. The whites are a darker gold than the white Burgundies.

## LOIRE WINES

The principle districts and their better known wines are:

**Anjou**
*White: Coteaux du Layon, Quarts de Chaume*
*Red and rosé: Saumur*

**Coteaux du Loir\***
*Sweetish white and rosé wines*

**Muscadet**
*Light, dry, white wines*

**Pouilly-sur-Loire**
*White: Pouilly Fumé*

**Sancerre**
*Dry white and rosé wines*

**Touraine**
*Red: Bourgeuil, Chinon*
*White: Vouvray*

\* Not to be confused with La Loire. In French, main rivers are feminine, tributaries masculine.

The Loire produces a considerable variety of whites and reds, which are meritorious if not world-beaters. The reds, Chinon and Bourgueil, are light and agreeable rather than distinguished. The sweet white Quarts de Chaume, from the Coteaux du Layon however, have been compared to a good Sauternes. The most stylish white wines come from the Upper Loire, Blanc Fumé de Pouilly or Pouilly Fumé (not to be confused with Pouilly Fuissé)—dry, delicate, round and flinty flavoured—and so do the lesser whites, simply called Pouilly-sur-Loire.

Sancerre provides much white wine, which must have an alcoholic strength of 10.5% to carry the name. From the Middle Loire come the Saumur wines, white, crisp and still or sparkling—the local people will try to persuade you that the sparkling ones are as good as Champagne.

From near the mouth of the Loire comes Muscadet, very dry and yet flowery. It has become immensely popular with (and through) visitors to Brittany from all over the world, especially as an accompaniment to sea-food.

## ALSACE WINES

Known by the name of the grape, the principal ones being:
RIESLING
*Full flavoured wine, not too sweet*
SYLVANER
*Produces lighter, slightly greenish wines, good for summer meals*
TRAMINER
*Mellow, soft, fruity flavour, and fragrant bouquet*
GERWURZTRAMINER
*A Traminer with a particularly rich bouquet*
TOKAY D'ALSACE (PINOT GRIS)
*Fruity dry or medium dry wine*
MUSCAT
*Fruity dry or medium dry wine*
PINOT BLANC

Alsace now produces considerable quantities of white wine, which have gained in popularity in recent years. They have a German rather than a French quality and are generally put into German-shaped bottles. The Rieslings and Sylvaners particularly resemble fairly closely the wines made from the same grapes along the Rhine. They are, in the main, full-bodied and fruity. The Traminer is generally dry and aromatic, but less spicey than the Gerwürztraminer (the prefix indicates the spiciness); the latter is a full and fragrant wine, recommended with paté, smoked salmon, Lobster Thermidor. The Muscat is an oddity: its powerful bouquet suggests a sweet wine, yet it is dry and has a piquancy entirely its own. Pinot Blanc d'Alsace is full-flavoured, a wine to drink right through a meal. There is also a wine named after the charming little town of Riquewihr—cheap and cheerful for a party.

*Muscadet ranges from dry to rich, fruity, and tasting of muscat grapes.*

# WHITE WINES OF GERMANY

*Some of the finest, the most delectable white wines in the world come from the beautiful vineyards along the borders of the Rhine and are known as Hock in English. The wines of Moselle and Franconia are often lighter.*

## HOCKS

from the districts of:

**Rheingau**
*Schloss Johannisberg\*, Winkel,
Oestrich, Erbach,
Eltville, Rudesheimer*

**Rheinhessen**
*Niersteiner Domtal,
Niersteiner Auflangen\*,
Dienheimer, Oppenheimer,
Mettenheimer, Laubenheimer*

**Nahe**
*Bad Kreuznach, Niederhauser,
Schloss Bockelheim*

**The Palatinate**
*Deidesheimer, Wachenheimer,
Bad Durkheimer*

## MOSELLES

*from the area of the Moselle, and the
Saar and Ruwer Rivers:
Bernkasteler Riesling,
Bernkasteler Doktor\*,
Bernkasteler Doktor und Graben,
Trittenheimer, Piesporter,
Brauneberger, Zeltinger*

## FRANCONIAN WINES

*from the district about Würzburg on
the River Main:
Steinwein, Iphofen, Randersacker,
Würzburg (Leisten)*

\* = very fine and very costly

This table groups together the three main types of German wine, the chief areas from which they come, and gives the names of just a few of the individual wines within each type. Since there are 10,000 vineyards, and over 150,000 wine growers, German wines are a very complicated subject, especially as there can be great variety even within one vineyard. However, here is a little more detail.

## HOCKS

The name 'Hock' is an anglicized diminutive of Hockheim, the old city three miles upstream on the River Main before it joins the Rhine.

It was at Hockheim, in 1850, that Queen Victoria gave her name to a vineyard providing her choice of wine— Koningen-Viktoria-Berg, and it may still be bought in Britain at a reasonable price.

From the Rheingau, the area to which the Hockheim vineyards belong, come the finest and costliest of Hocks, full-bodied, flavoury, delicately fragrant and long-living. Almost all of them are made from the Reisling grape—which is very often named on the label on the bottle, and usually means that the contents of that bottle will be expensive!

The route below the Rheingau vineyards is surrounded by some of the most splendid scenery in Europe, and winds through villages of great charm, all of them bearing the names of famous wines —Johannisberg, Winkel, Oestrich, Erbach, Eltville and Rudesheim. This last is a very popular summer resort, famed for its succulent sausages and the vigour of its singing in the gay *wein stubes*.

Rheinhessen, on the left bank of the Rhine, is a larger area than Rheingau, stretching along the right bank of the river, and the Hocks which it produces are rather less delicate. Maybe its greatest claim to fame is that it yields the best-known and (certainly in Britain) most popular of all German wines— Liebfraumilch.

The name comes from the Liebfrauen-stift vineyard, close to the old church at Worms called the Liebfrauenkirche, but it has been freely used for blends of wines coming from places that may be far away from Worms. Even so, a remarkably good quality has been maintained over many years. Now, under new laws taking effect from the 1971 vintage, Lieb-fraumilch must be a blend of grapes grown in Rheinhessen, Nahe or the Palatinate, not just any German white wine, and this, unfortunately, is bound to put the price up.

Almost as popular as Liebfraumilch in Britain and other countries, too, is Niersteiner, from Nierstein, also in Rheinhessen. (The name of a village or area with 'er' added to it becomes the name of its wine: Nierstein/Niersteiner, Bernkastel/Bernkasteler.) All the neighbourhood families depend, directly or indirectly, on the vines, and as there are some 500 individual owners of vineyards, quality naturally varies. At the relatively cheap end of the scale is Niersteiner Domtal (Domtal is the name of a district, not a vineyard), which is fresh and agreeably flowery. Like other inexpensive Niersteiners, it is a good companion for fish, and may be drunk right through a meal by anyone who prefers white wine to red. At the other end of the price scale is the rare and beautiful wine from a single vineyard, like Niersteiner Auflangen Riesling Feinste Auslese. The German words are a brief 'biography' of the wine: Niersteiner is the district, Auflangen the name of the vineyard, and 'Riesling Feinste Auslese' means 'Made from finest selected bunches of Riesling grapes'.

Wines from the Palatinate are heavier in flavour and bouquet than other Rhine wines. Their prices vary very much: a Deidesheimer, for example, can be very reasonable, and a Wachenheimer Gerumpel Riesling Trockenbeeren Auslese can be more than ten times more expensive. The latter wine is a rarity, made from selected grapes, virtually picked one by one; the last three words in the name tell you, in fact, that the wine is made from specially selected bunches of Riesling grapes which have been allowed to shrivel like raisins. The Riesling is used for these splendid wines, but the predominant grape in Rheinhessen is the Sylvaner.

## MOSELLES

The quantities of German wine may be tiny compared with those from other European wine-producing areas, but the variety is really remarkable. The greatest of the Hocks have a luscious, heady opulence, whereas the Moselles are summery, fresh and crisp, so that they often produce a tingle on the tongue. In colour, they are a lighter gold than the Hocks, and have a faint green tinge. Their acidity is quite high and their alcoholic content fairly low.

The Moselle vineyards are on mountain slopes, terraced to hold the slatey soil, and work is hard, because the use of machinery on the steep hillsides is almost

*Tall-stemmed Hock glass with a rounded bowl which should be clear to show the delicate colour of the wine.*

impossible. The Riesling is virtually the only grape grown in the whole area. Most of the familiar wines come from the Middle Moselle, between Trittenheim and Alf—this is the home of Bernkasteler, Piesporter, Brauneberger, Wehlener and Zeltinger.

Bernkasteler Riesling is one of the most popular, not only because it is light and inexpensive, but because Bernkastel itself is such a delightful town. After King Edward VII's doctor had recommended Bernkasteler Doktor to him, it achieved such fame that the demand unfortunately became impossible to meet. However, it is possible to find a Bernkasteler Doktor und Graben (Graben is the vineyard next to Doktor).

And there are some very admirable characteristic and reasonably-priced Bernkastel wines available—Deinhard's popular Bernkasteler Green Label, for example, which is comparable in price and quality to an equally well known brand-name Hock—Liebfraumilch Crown of Crowns, from Langenbach. Wines from Piesport are also favourites abroad, particularly Piesporter Goldtropfchen. Wines from this district tend to display a tarry flavour and this gives them fullness.

## FRANCONIAN WINES

The best known of all, outside Germany, is the Steinwein from Würzburg. It is dry, even austere, with a more robust flavour but a fainter bouquet than other German white wines. It is bottled in a flat, oval green flask, a *bocksbütel*. Generally, though, Franconian wines are light, delicate, fragrant and dry to medium dry. The grape most used in the area is the Sylvaner.

## OTHER DISTRICTS

The provinces of Baden and Württemberg, and the area about the Bodensee, near to the Swiss border, produce between them a quarter of Germany's output of wine, using a mixture of Riesling and Sylvaner grapes, but almost all of it is drunk locally.

**Main Types of Grape**
RIESLING: *Used in making almost all the fine Moselles and Rheingau Hocks.*
SYLVANER: *Used for cheaper wines. Has very pronounced bouquet and taste. Predominant Rheinhessen grape.*
TRAMINER: *Used particularly in the Palatinate, for full, scented wines tending to sweetness.*

**Recent Good Vintages**
1964, 1966, 1971

# WHITE WINES OF THE WORLD

*From Portugal to Hungary in Europe, from Australia and South Africa, and from the Americas, comes a wide variety of white wines.*

## PORTUGAL

Portugal's Vinhos Verdes are fresh, slightly sparkling wines which charm the eye as well as the palate, are greenish in tinge but they are only 'green' in the sense of 'new'. In actual fact Vinhos Verdes can be white (familiar brand names are Casal Garcia and Lagosta), red or rosé. They come from the Minho province, north of Oporto, more particularly from the vicinity of Monção and Viana do Castelo; a distinctive feature of the vineyards is that the grapes are grown on trellises or even up trees. These wines can be very dry, almost astringent, but some of them, the exported ones, are distinctly less so—to suit the 'average' palate. The best, chilled, make admirable aperitifs as does the still Vila Real from a wine growing district near the rolling slopes producing Port. This can be dry enough to make you sit up, if flagging. At the other end of the sugar scale, there is a good sweet dessert wine, Moscatel de Setubal with a distinctive aroma.

## SPAIN

Spain, is perhaps noted more for its red than white table wines, but there are some excellent Rioja whites, a dry white of merit from Valdespenas and, for those who like it pretty sweet, a Muscatel.

## ITALY

Best known Italian white wines, outside Italy at any rate, are Verdicchio, from Marche, medium dry and agreeable; Orvieto, from Umbria, generally to be found in flat-bottomed wicker bottles; Soave, best-known of the lot, fresh and flavoury; from Verona, Lacrima Christi, delicate and with a hint (sometimes more of a nudge) of sweetness; Frascati; and, from Montefiascone, the oddly named Est! Est! Est!, golden yellow and fruity. The legend is that a 12th century bishop sent his steward ahead with the instructions to mark Est! (short for *vinum bonum est*—the wine is good) on the doors of taverns where it was so. He became over-enthusiastic.

## AUSTRIA

Much of the best wine comes from around the lovely old town of Krems, some 70 miles from Vienna, and from Durnstein, where some good wines are made from the Sylvaner, Riesling, Traminer and Veltliner grapes, often with a tingle on the tongue and a deceptive suggestion of lightness in alcohol. It has been claimed for them that they are less likely than other wines to induce a hangover. Familiar to travellers are the Schluck, which can be 'prickly' and is generally medium dry—delicious on a very hot day—and Gumboldskirchner, from south of Vienna, made from the Traminer and the Rotgipfler grape peculiar to Austria. A good 'middle taste' wine.

## SWITZERLAND

Swiss white wines tend to resemble the lighter and drier Moselles, often have a light sparkle, and are usually drunk young. Fendant, a fairly full wine, comes from some of the highest vineyards in Europe, in the Valais, and Neuchatel from the shores of the lake of that name.

## YUGOSLAVIA

The fabulously successful Lutomer Riesling, named simply from district and grape is medium dry, fruity, and dependable. 'Tiger Milk' is a sweet white wine made from late picked grapes.

## HUNGARY

Hungary's chief claim to wine fame is its incomparable Tokay, golden, lusciously sweet and deliciously flavoured. It has been compared in quality, as a dessert wine, with Sauternes. The term 'puttonyos' indicates the degree of sweetness. The best and most luscious, such as Tokay Aszu, 5 puttonyos, 1964, is superb. Balatoni Riesling, light straw coloured and full, somewhat sweet.

## EASTERN MEDITERRANEAN

The Lebanon produces a full dry white something like a Graves. Greece, a dry white which is aromatic but free of resin, which makes it acceptable to non-Greeks. Israel has a white called 'Hock', as indeed has Cyprus, and palatable enough it is; Rumania, a medium dry from the Perla grape grown beside the Tirnave River.

## SOUTH AFRICA

A variety of attractive white wines come from South Africa, some of those coming from the Paarl and Stellenbosch somewhat resembling white Burgundies. (Paarl is in Cape Province, and is the centre of the Co-operative Wine Growers' Association of South Africa). Another area for white wine is Tulbagh. Some excellent Hock-type wines are produced, and also dessert wines made from the Muscat grape and from the famous Constantia vineyards, where the first wine was produced in South Africa in 1659.

South African wines are generally of good quality, carefully controlled and well produced.

## AUSTRALIA

Australia's list is long, many wines called by the grape name after the grower's name, others using the French district terms such as 'White Burgundy' and 'Sauternes'—with the explanation that "the use of generic descriptions is still appreciated by many as an aid to description". Among the many palatable and consistent whites exported are Gramp's Orlando Barossa Riesling, the cheapest and, at a higher quality and price level, Lindemann's Coolalta White Burgundy.

## NORTH AMERICA

Canada and the United States both produce white wine. Most of Canada's production comes from the area around Niagara, and a little comes from British Columbia. Most tend to be rather sweet, though Château Gai is slightly less so. The United States produces a fine variety of wines, from very sweet to very dry. But anyone familiar with the sweeter Sauternes of France will be rather surprised to find that the white wines of the United States described as 'Sauternes' are comparatively dry. California alone has about 200 wineries, producing splendid wines, able to hold their own with the best French wines. Unfortunately very little of it is exported! The Californian wines are usually described by the grape from which they have been made or their region of origin, like Napa Valley, Sonoma, Santa Clara, Livermore Valley and Fresno. Apart from California, the other important wine producing area is around New York State, which produces some fine white wines and especially sparkling one. One of the best wines from the United States is called Emerald Riesling.

## BRITAIN

Finally, don't laugh, even England with its damp climate, manages to produce its own white wines, notably Hambledon, estate bottled by Sir Guy Salisbury-Jones and made from grapes grown in his Hambledon vineyards, hinting at a dry and elegant Vouvray. It is thought that the Romans introduced vineyards to Britain. Wine was produced until Henry VIII dissolved the monastries which were the major wine producers.

# CHAMPAGNE AND SPARKLING WINE

*Champagne is one of the most versatile drinks—there's always a good excuse to open a bottle for a party or as a very special aperitif.*

Champagne is still superlative among all the sparkling wines. It has a cachet unmatched by any other wine, and yet it is no longer the most expensive by any means. Even the really illustrious Champagnes—Laurent Perrier Cuvée Grand Siècle, selected from three best years blended together, or Moet & Chandon's Dom Perignon, or Diamant Bleu from Heidsieck Monopole—no longer begin to approach the most sought-after Clarets in price. In fact, they are liable to be a great deal cheaper than the first-growth Clarets of any year that matters. Even so, Champagne can never be cheap, because of the care given to its production and the time required for it to reach maturity.

## WHEN TO DRINK CHAMPAGNE

One of the great things about Champagne is that it's *always* good to drink—at breakfast, mid-morning, lunch, mid-afternoon, at weddings and christenings, as an aperitif, with dinner, or to soothe the nerves on a 'plane. It makes a party go. It's for toasting, for launching ships, for seeing in the New Year. It makes an occasion: it never needs to wait for one.

## THE CHAMPAGNE AREA

The Champagne area forms a rough circle round Epernay, in north-east France (to the north and north-east of Paris). Many of the famous Champagne Houses are located there, or in Rheims. Owing to its geographical location, the area has been much fought over; the windmill at Verenzay, for example, which is owned by Heidsieck Monopole, was used as an observation post by both sides during World War I. Even so, vinification has survived from ancient times in this most northerly wine-growing district in France.
Champagne as we know it today owes much to two people: Dom Perignon and Madame Clicquot. Dom Perignon, a contemporary of Louis XIV, became Cellarer of the Abbey of Hautvilliers in 1670, but the records of the Abbey were, alas, lost in the French Revolution. However, it is generally accepted that Dom Perignon transformed the wine from one reputed to be pinkish and fermenting unpredictably, so that bottle explosions were not uncommon, into a mature aristocrat, well-balanced, golden and sparkling. Important factors in this evolution were the production of a strong bottle and the use of a cork wired onto the bottle instead of wood and hemp as a stopper. (Madame Clicquot's part in the story comes a little later).

## THE MAKING OF CHAMPAGNE

Champagne is actually made from more black grapes than white. Under the strict rules governing its making, only three types of grape are permissible: Pinot Noir and Meunier (black) and Chardonnay (white). Some Champagne is made from white grapes only, and the resulting wine, which is rather more delicate and lighter in style, is referred to as *Blanc de Blancs*. Pink (or Rosé) Champagne is produced by allowing the juice of the black grapes to remain in contact with the skins for a few hours. To give you an idea of why Champagne costs so much, here is a brief outline of its manufacture.
In the vineyards, great care is taken (by means of expert inspection by women) to ensure that the selected grapes are undamaged when they go to the presses, so that the white juice from the black grapes is not coloured by the skins. In the early stages, the making of Champagne is similar to the vinification of white wines elsewhere. The 'must' (the clear white juice) is put into casks, where the first fermentation takes place. Then it is 'racked'—transferred to new casks—during the winter, leaving behind the sediment cast off during fermentation. The new wines of different pressings are then blended to obtain one standard wine. This 'assembly' (*cuvée*) of wine requires a highly skilled operation, in the charge of the Chef de Caves, who is consequently responsible for the style and taste of the finished product.
In spring the blends for the year's vintage (if any) wines and non-vintage wines are transferred to bottling vats, a little sugar syrup is dissolved in the wine (*liqueur de tirage*), yeast cultures are added (*levurage*), and the wine is bottled with a temporary—perhaps a crown—cork. A second fermentation then takes place and the bottles are left in the cellars to mature, usually for two or three years if the Champagne is non-vintage, perhaps for five if it is vintage. Two important '*méthode champenoise*' processes are '*remuage*'— the gradual tilting of the bottle and regular expert rotating to ensure that the sediment eventually lies on the cork, and '*dégorgement*', which means the disgorging of the sediment. Today, this is usually achieved by freezing the neck of the bottle; the pressure when the stopper is removed ejects the small lump of frozen wine containing the sediment. The old method involved the use of the thumb, and it demanded a high degree of skill. This is where Madame Clicquot comes in. Left a widow at 27, she carried on her father's business (founded in 1772), and discovered the essential principle of *remuage*.
The gap left by the ejected sediment is topped up with wine and sugar syrup (without which Champagne would be undrinkably dry). The *dosage*, as it's called, varies according to whether the wine is to be *Brut, sec, demi-sec,* or *doux*:
DRY: *Brut, Natur, Extra Dry, Extra Sec, Trés Sec*
MEDIUM DRY: *Dry, Sec*
MEDIUM SWEET: *Demi-Sec*
SWEET: *Doux, Rich*
The words describing the various types of Champagne tend to sound drier than the wines actually are. Drier Champagne is currently in fashion and the British prefer it, but the French enjoy sweet Champagne at the end of a meal. Vintage or non-vintage Extra Dry Champagne is delicious as an aperitif, or at the beginning of a meal, especially with hors d'oeuvres and fish, and a Demi-Sec or Doux wine goes well with the sweet course.
A wine from the Champagne area is Crémant—not so sparkling as usual, and with a delicate flavour.

## VINTAGE CHAMPAGNE

Vintage Champagne is made from the blending of the wines made from the vine crop of an exceptionally good year (which is stamped on corks and labels). It is probably at its best when it is between 7 and 12 years old, and it should be richer and more full of flavour than the non-vintage kind. The demand for it is so great (with Britain and the USA well in the lead) that a large amount of it is drunk when it's younger—most of the famous Houses introduced the 1966 in 1972, for example, because the 1964 vintage had largely disappeared. A very old Champagne may or may not be worth drinking. In recent years I've sampled a 1911, which was deep yellow, hardly sparkling, but not disagreeable, and a 1926 (a good year) which was still working (bubbling) industriously, and which had remained fruity and delicious. Some of the vintage Champagne from one year is kept for blending with the wine of other years to make the non-vintage Champagne. The aim here is to blend different years that are consistent in flavour and quality, and this can be done with such skill that only an expert could distinguish the result as a non-vintage wine. The only problem is that Champagne can deteriorate over a period of time (say, 4 or 5 years), and since non-vintage Champagne carries no year, there is just the chance that you could be drinking a wine past its prime. Drink non-vintage Champagne when it's young, and don't lay it down. (There's not much likelihood of doing that, anyway, in these days of high demand.)

## OPENING A BOTTLE

After all the care that has gone into its making, Champagne deserves—and requires—thoughtful opening. Don't jiggle the bottle; put two glasses ready in case it's lively, and have a clean napkin handy, to mop any spills and—more importantly—to protect your fingers from wire; do not point the cork at people, or at valuables—or at your chin. Remove the foil and the wire holding the properly 'aimed' bottle with the napkin, then grasp the cork, and turn *the bottle* steadily. (N.B. The bottle, not the cork.) The aim is not to produce a cannonade, or to waste half the bottle, but rather to hear a very, very gentle 'phut'.

## HOW TO SERVE

Champagne should be served cold but not iced, so don't leave it in the fridge too long. Its ideal temperature is about 9 °C (48 °F). Drink it from a tulip-shaped glass (see page 62), or any ordinary wine glass if you haven't any of the tulip ones, but preferably not out of the saucer-like coupe, which is a silly shape, when the idea is that you should be able to see the lovely gay bubbles rising up through the golden liquid. Unlike most French wines, Champagne is known by the names of the Houses who make it, rather than by the names of the vineyards. The House names are referred to as 'Grandes Marques'.

*Cool, fresh, fragrant white wine turns the simplest summer fare into a feast.*

Some of the great Champagne Houses: Bollinger, Heidsieck, Heidsieck Dry Monopole, Irroy, Krug, Lanson, Laurent-Perrier, Moet & Chandon, Mumm, Perrier-Jouet, Pol Roger, Pommery & Greno, Roederer, Taittinger and Veuve Clicquot.

**Recent good vintages**
1961, 1962, 1964, 1966, 1969

## OTHER SPARKLING WINES

These are all excellent for parties, or as a base for summer coolers. Although none of them may be called Champagne, they are made either by the *méthode champenoise*, or by secondary fermentation in closed tanks, and they come mainly from France, Italy and Germany. France produces a number from districts other than Champagne, notably the Loire and the Rhône.

**The Loire's** Sparkling Saumur has enjoyed wide popularity for a long time, particularly for parties. It is clean and fresh, and much of it is somewhat sweet, though there are dry ones, like Saumur Soleil. Sparkling Vouvray is also rather sweeter than Champagne, but it is admirable for 'young' occasions, and much used at weddings, although some people find too much of it rather 'head-achy'.

**Rhône's** deservedly popular light sparkler, Blanc de Blancs, comes from Seyssel, a small town on the Rhône near Annecey. Strictly speaking, it is an Haut-Savoie wine, and it makes a delicious aperitif.

**Burgundy,** too, supplies some sparkling wines, both white (extra dry) and red, which have had a small but devoted following for a long time.

**Germany:** production of Germany's sparkling Hock and Moselle, called *Sekt*, has soared in recent years—from under 10 million bottles in 1952 to 135 million in 1969. One of the leading wines is Henkell-Trocken, from Wiesbaden. Others, whether from the Rhine or the Moselle, range from dry to sweetish and appear under a variety of names, among them 'Sparkling Crown of Crowns', 'Schloss Reingarten' 'Kupferberg' and 'Sparkling Hock Deinhard Cabinet'.

**Italy's** Asti Spumante is claimed to be the only sparkling wine which benefits more from secondary fermentation in tank than it would from the *méthode champenoise*, as this better preserves the fragrance of the Muscat grape. Spumante is sweet, but it is possible to obtain a dryish Asti sparkler.

**Portugal:** The region of Vinhos Verdes produces the unique red and white 'green' wines (the rosé is dealt with on Page 42)—the 'green' in this case referring to the wine's youth and liveliness and not its colour. Vinhos Verdes are light and fragrant and they all have a slight suggestion of sparkle. Other sound sparkling wines come from the Bairrada region, from Oporto, and particularly from Lamego, on the edge of the Douro region, all of them produced by the *méthode champenoise*.

**Australia** produces some excellent sparkling wines, the most distinguished being Seppelt's Great Western Imperial Reserve.

**The USA** has two main wine-producing areas, from both of which come sparkling wines—California and New York State. Some are made by the Champagne method, some by the *cuve clos* method, and some have carbon dioxide pumped into the wine, but these must carry the description 'carbonated'. The Taylor wineries are the largest 'Champagne' producers in the States.

# VIN ROSÉ – LIGHT AND GAY

*Rosé undoubtedly has a tremendous popular appeal, despite the views of the anti-Rosé brigade, who insist that it is neither one thing nor the other. Certainly it isn't a long-living wine, and it is best drunk young. But it undoubtedly suggests gaiety, so how do we make the very most of it?*

## HOW TO SERVE

First of all, any Rosé, even Tavel should be chilled. And as one of its attractions is visual, it should be served in a glass that does justice to its pretty colour. A tulip-shaped glass—the kind used for Champagne—is one idea, or, if you happen to have any, glasses with hollow stems; these are especially suitable if the Rosé is sparkling. In any case, serve it in glasses with stems, because it's certainly best drunk to the last drop while it's still cool. The sweeter Rosés can become quite flabby if they are too warm.

So, Rosé is a drink for any time and anywhere, but I recommend a warm, sunny morning in a garden—among roses. And if you do find yourself landed with a less-than-interesting Rosé, it can always be used to make the basis of a colourful wine cup—or just add a strawberry, or a leaf or two of young mint, to give it a more refreshing aroma. And if it's a really hot day, put in a clink or two of ice.

They are lighter in alcoholic strength than other wines, but they're by no means 'teetotal'.

## HOW ROSE IS MADE

Rosés (the best anyway) are produced in the same way as other wines, the difference being that they are made from black grapes, the skins of which are removed from the 'must' when the wine is beginning to take colour and before it becomes really red. There are pink wines made by mixing red and white wines, and even some made by the addition of cochineal to white wine—a disreputable practice, though the dye is harmless enough. However, no one buying a Rosé from a reliable shop or restaurant need worry about this possibility.

## WHICH ONE?

Today there is a wide choice of Rosés, both still and sparkling. I shall mention my own personal favourite first—Tavel, from the Rhône, generally the driest, most robust, and, at its best, certainly the most distinguished, of them all. The fullness is the more surprising since the wine comes from soil so barren—sand, lime and loose flints—that it is hard to imagine vines growing on it at all. And Tavel is certainly not a wine to be thought of as having no kick.

Generally more popular are the sweeter Anjou Rosés, from one of the most beautiful stretches of the château-guarded Middle Loire. They are usually listed as medium dry—like the Cabernet, for example. The Loire also produces sparkling Rosés. In fact, Rosés are made almost everywhere that black grapes are grown: there's even a new, slightly sweet, sparkling Pink Rosé made from Muscat grapes, called Lily the Pink—sounds very merry!

Burgundy and Bordeaux both produce Rosés—including a Beaujolais Rosé—which tend to be somewhat dryer than those of Anjou. And some good Rosés come from Provence—sprightly ones,

hinting at Mediterranean sunshine. Among them is the light-medium Pradel Rosé from Villeneuve-Coubet and (also French bottled) Bandol Domaine du Val d'Arène; the 1969 is full and well-balanced, one of the few (apart from Tavel) which can be drunk through a meal. Finally, still in France, there is a Rosé from the Montpellier-Beziers district, called Pelure d'Oignon, which means 'onion skin'!

**Portugal** today exports very considerable quantities of Rosé wines, most of them still or slightly sparkling rather than fully sparkling. Of the slightly sparkling, the most widely promoted one has been Mateus Rosé, contained in attractive, Franconian-style bottles. The wine is, frankly, not exceptional, but amiable enough, darkish for a Rosé, medium, and, in fact, middle-of-the-road, with a tingle rather than a sparkle and handy enough if you are in a quandary about what to serve at a party which is not likely to be too demanding. Similar to it is Faisca. Another agreeable prickly pink Rosé is Quinta do Roi, which comes from Bussaco and may well have been enjoyed by Wellington's soldiers during the Peninsular War. Some brand-name Rosés are available either still or sparkling—'Justina', for example.

**Spain** supplies considerable quantities of Rosé wine, too, most of the exports bearing brand names or the Spanish word 'Rosado'. A Rosado from Rioja can be pleasantly dry and crisp, and also less insipid than some of the cheaper brands.

**Hungary**—Horgony Rosé is medium-dry and reasonably priced.

**South Africa's** most notable contribution to the river of Rosé flowing round the world today is the Twee Jongezeller ('Two Bachelors'), from the beautiful Tulbagh Valley in Cape Province.

In **Australia** the demand for Rosé wines is not very considerable, possibly because the alcoholic strength is less than in other wines. They are usually marketed under the names of the grower and the grape, the Grenache generally producing the best wine. Grenache Rosé, for example, is light, young and medium as to sweetness. There is also Seppelt's Spritzig, and the word is descriptive of the slight sparkle in Portuguese Rosés, to which this one has some resemblance.

**The United States.** From the Paul Masson vineyards in California comes a Grenache Rosé which has the onion-skin colour of a good Tavel, though it is sweeter.

*For hot days, add a strawberry or mint leaf to chilled vin rosé.*

# A PERFECT END TO THE MEAL - A GLASS OF PORT OR BRANDY

*You would be denying yourself one of life's keener pleasures if you didn't try drinking one or the other straight at the end of the evening meal. A feeling of content and a loosening of the tongue becomes inevitable if you take the simple precaution of offering Brandy or Armagnac (which comes from France) or Port—vintage or non-vintage.*

## PORT

Port is made in Portugal, on the River Douro. It is a fortified wine—that is to say, the fermenting grape juice has brandy added to it. Start with a 1960 vintage Port and alter your life. And if you do buy a vintage Port, remember not to drink it for at least five days after you get it home. Vintage Port throws a deep sediment which has to settle—so open it without shaking or moving the bottle from the position in which it was left. The last third must be strained through a handkerchief, leaving about one eighth of crust and silt in the bottle. It is a pity to waste your money and spoil your ultimate pleasure by ignoring this simple rule: a good glass of vintage Port should be as clear as clear if you hold it up to the light. The difference in taste between clear and cloudy is immediately apparent, even to people who have never drunk Port before. Vintage Port has an alcoholic strength of 20°.

A special Port decanter is unnecessary—any glass jug will do, since a bottle has a way of vanishing in spite of the best intentions of economy, even when it is shared by only two normally abstemious people. Our Victorian forebears used to forbid Port to their womenfolk and made them retire after dinner while the gentlemen indulged. This sensible if hypocritical practice was intended to conserve supplies and still occurs in some country houses today.

The snag about drinking vintage Port is that the price of even a recent year starts almost level with Whisky and escalates to the cost of a set of new tyres for, say, a Cockburn 1904. On the other hand, there are the Tawny and Ruby Ports which are blended from different years and vineyards, although Ruby is sometimes of one particular vintage. Their alcoholic strength is very little less than 20°, and they won't disturb your economy much.

Tawny Port is aged in cask, causing it to lose colour, and is bottled free of the sediment that sinks to the bottom of the barrel. Ruby Port is bottled before the colour has a chance to fade. It is prudent to buy those Ports that have been blended by the shipper in Portugal and that bear his name rather than the blends of non-Portuguese wine-merchants.

**When to drink vintage Port**
1945, '48, '50, '55, '58—now to late '70s.
1960—from 1973
1963, '66—from 1980
1967—from 1978

## COGNAC

Cognac is a district in France, north of Bordeaux, which produces a special Brandy. This region used to belong to the kings of England until the fifteenth century, when the French took it back while the English weren't looking during the Wars of the Roses. Think of all the customs duty England has had to pay since!

Brandy is matured in oak casks for a number of years—well-aged blends may be VSOP (Very Special Old Pale).

The process is slow and expensive. Ten barrels of white wine are needed to produce one barrel of Brandy, which in turn evaporates as it ages. The younger Brandies have a sharp fiery edge, which makes them less suitable for drinking after a meal and more worthy of added ginger ale or soda. In its natural state Brandy is a pale straw colour: the sweet, dark-hued products are adjustments made with sugar and caramel.

After graduating from VSOP Brandy it is worth the experiment to buy a Brandy of a pre-war year; you may never be able to afford another bottle but the memory will be well worth the price.

PS Mistrust anyone, in a restaurant or elsewhere, who goes through the mumbo-jumbo of heating a Brandy glass over a flame.

## ARMAGNAC

This is the only other Brandy in the world to compare with Cognac. It is darker usually and has a distinctive flavour highly prized by some, who prefer it to its neighbour. The difference is partly due to the process of distilling which is at a lower strength (53° compared to Brandy's 70°) and to the casks, made from the local 'sappy' oak which ages the spirit much faster. Up to 1905 Armagnac was blended with Cognac to give the latter colour and the appearance of great age and smoothness.

The smell of Armagnac is very pungent and the savour stays in the mouth for a long time; it is very dry because no sugar is added. The difference in its strength aside, Armagnac is preferable to most cheaper Cognacs at the same price level.

## BRANDIES ROUND THE WORLD

Many countries produce forms of brandy and some of the finest, after the Cognac of France, come from South Africa. California in the United States now actually produces more Brandy than France.

Australia also has a flourishing Brandy trade and now even exports about a quarter of her production.

## GLASSES AND DECANTERS

There is no need to buy those expensive balloon glasses for your Cognac or Armagnac: if your nose is long it will rest on the far rim and you will have to almost break your neck in tilting your head back to swallow. Nor do you need to acquire any special glass for Port. A small tulip-shaped wine-glass will do fine for either drink, although some think that a Port glass should properly have straight sides.

Recently exaggeratedly large brandy glasses have become fashionable but these tend to be difficult to handle and demand extra large measures.

# LIQUEURS

*These are alcohol, flavoured and usually sweetened, or sometimes distilled from fruit or nuts. Liqueurs are usually drunk straight after a meal.*

**Advocaat (Holland):** Brandy, eggs and vanilla. Sweet and widely popular.

**Anisette (France):** Colourless, aniseed flavoured. Similar in taste to *Goldwasser* from Germany, which is laced with particles of gold leaf.

**Apricot Brandy (many countries):** Speaks for itself. Sweet.

**Aquavit (Denmark):** Colourless grain or potato spirit, flavoured with caraway seeds. Very potent and fiery. Usually tossed down at a gulp before a meal. Good for combatting long Scandinavian winters.

**Bénédictine (France):** Probably the oldest and still one of the best liqueurs. First distilled by the Benedictine monks in the early sixteenth century as a medicine for malaria—and a tonic to revive tired clergy. Flavouring includes arnica, hyssop, vanilla, cinnamon, coriander, nutmeg, mace, saffron and cardamon.

**Calvados (France):** Apple Brandy from Normandy. Sold at six years old or over—making it superior to the American Applejack.

**Crème de Cassis (France):** Very sweet and blackcurranty. Often confused with the non-alcoholic cordial called Sirop de Cassis.

**Chartreuse (France):** Made by Carthusian monks near Grenoble. Comes in two colours—green and yellow. The latter is less potent and much sweeter.

**Cherry Brandy (many countries):** Speaks for itself. Very sweet.

**Cointreau (France):** Colourless, orange-flavoured liqueur, similar to *Grand Marnier*.

**Crème de Cacao (France):** Very sweet, tasting strongly of chocolate. Made from cocoa beans.

**Crème de Menthe (France):** Strongly peppermint-flavoured. Usually drunk well iced.

*Cointreau*

*Crème de Cacao*

*Green Chartreuse*

*Blue Curacao*

*Van der Hum*

*Southern Comfort*

**Curacao (West Indies):** Similar to Cointreau. The colour is either golden or a delicate blue.

**Drambuie (Scotland):** Whisky, honey and herbs. The recipe is said to have been a gift to an ancestor of the present proprietors from that noted drinker, Bonnie Prince Charlie.

**Forbidden Fruit (America):** Orange and honey flavoured, with a Brandy base. The colour is a beautiful golden brown.

**Framboise (France):** Colourless, dry, and distilled from raspberries. Delicious served chilled or otherwise.

**Galliano (Italy):** Pale yellow. Somewhat similar in flavour to Strega.

**Grand Marnier** (see *Cointreau*.)

**Grappa** (see *Marc*).

**Kirsch (Germany):** Colourless. Distilled from the juice and kernels of German cherries. Extra dry and good. *Maraschino* is similar but sweet.

**Kahlua (Mexico):** Like Creme de Cacao, made with cocoa beans and grain spirit. Popular in the USA and good poured over ice-cream.

**Kummel (Baltic States):** Vodka and caraway seeds. Fine if you like caraway seeds.

**Marc (France):** Made from the pressing of skins, pips and stems of grapes of the Burgundy and Champagne districts which have already been pressed to make wine. Similar to *Grappa* (Italy).

**Mirabelle (France):** Plum Brandy

from golden-yellow plums. Resembles *Slivovitz* (Yugoslavia), but without the latter's fiery quality.

**Sloe Gin (Britain):** Sugar, sloes and gin, and very good indeed, especially for people who don't drink but who need something sweet to hold at parties and festivities.

**Southern Comfort (USA):** Made from Bourbon and peaches, presumably to console the South for defeat in the American Civil War.

**Strega (Italy):** Said to be flavoured with aromatic herbs and barks, but some people claim that it's more like very sweet varnish!

**Tia Maria (Jamaica):** Rum flavoured with coffee beans. It will transform the dullest vanilla ice-cream into a treat.

**Van der Hum (South Africa):** The colour is russet brown and the flavour a rich tangerine.

*Calvados*          *Cherry Brandy*

*Crème de Cassis*          *Kahlua*          *Strega*

# COFFEE – PLUS A DASH

*No-one who has ever woken up in Paris to smell the aroma of the morning's coffee rising from the courtyard of the hotel is ever likely to forget it. In the same way, a fine cup of coffee after dinner rates as a first class drink if properly made. But too often, it turns out to be bitter and insipid. Here's how to make it well, and how to add a dash of something stronger.*

## METHOD OF MAKING

First of all, coffee must be properly made. The usual methods, in a variety of machinery, are straining, percolating and filtering. Putting coffee in a pot, adding boiling water and straining the resulting infusion is the most popular but disperses all the aroma. Further, any instrument or device made of metal or glass which is elaborate and difficult to work should be given away. Buy filter bags and a cone to rest the paper wafer in. Have your coffee ground to the right degree—very fine if you have your own grinder. Put $1\frac{1}{4}$ oz (approx. 40 grams) per pint in the cone filter sitting on a pot that's warming on the stove. Pour in boiling water, measured in a cup. Repeat until the correct number of cupfuls is in the bottom of the pot. The virtue of the paper filter is that the coffee is not itself boiled and acid ingredients are held back. It can even be successfully re-heated but NOT boiled.

The alternative method is to use a coffee-pot with a plunger. This works on almost the same principle as the filter. Put in $1\frac{1}{4}$ oz (approx. 40 grams) per pint of water. Pour on the boiling water. Stir. Let the coffee stand for three to five minutes. Depress the plunger and the coffee is made.

If you suffer from hard water, a water softener would improve out of recognition not only your coffee but also cooking generally (and bathing!). The next hurdle is the choice of coffee.

## THE COFFEE TO CHOOSE

In Europe the habit is to roast the beans more than is popular in Britain or America—hence the darker colour of the 'continental' coffees. Experiment with various fresh-roasted coffees until you find the one that suits you—and your water supply—best. Breakfast coffee sometimes doesn't go well after dinner, so have two kinds in store. Buy as little at a time as is practical: large amounts of ground coffee go stale very quickly. For dinner try Blue Mountain from Jamaica or Chagga from the volcanic lower slopes of Mount Meru. Ever since the day, so the story goes, when an Arab goatherd in the Yemen noticed that his goats perked up after eating the red berries of wild coffee, people have been overdoing the drinking of coffee at night, perking themselves up just before going to bed. The coffee is wrongly blamed for insomnia; moderation is the cure. The spread of coffee to Europe in the baggage of the Turkish army besieging Vienna in the seventeenth century was first noticed by a Polish officer called Kolschitzky, who was looting the camp left by the fleeing Turks. He set up the first coffee-shop in Vienna and from there the habit spread rapidly across Europe, first the French and then the Dutch growing the plant in their colonies for the export trade.

### Turkish coffee

Since coffee succeeded where Turkish troops failed to penetrate Western Europe, it is worth considering how the Turkish soldiers prepared it at home—particularly since the pulverized ingredient they used is now fairly easy to obtain. This can be made either in a copper Turkish copper pot, known as an *Ibrik*, or in a saucepan. Use pulverized coffee, obtainable from specialist coffee shops. For four people pour a standard cup and a half of water into a pan with six teaspoonsfuls of castor sugar. Bring to boiling point. Add three heaped dessertspoonfuls of very finely ground coffee. Bring to the boil three times. Take pan off the heat and add a few drops of cold water. With a spoon take a little of the froth from the surface of the coffee and put into each small coffee cup. Pour the coffee very slowly into the cup.

## COFFEE PLUS ALCOHOL

The popularity of coffee among the Moslem Turks and Arabs was as a substitute for alcohol, forbidden them by religion. In Christian countries, where no such prohibition exists, the invigorating properties of coffee are enhanced by the addition of alcohol. In Italy a slug of aniseed (*anis, anice*) ensures a pleasant wakefulness for the business of the later evening.

Call it Highland coffee if you lace it with a good dollop of a single-malt Whisky or Drambuie, café royal if you add Cognac, Carribean coffee with a fine Barbados Rum, Danish with Aquavit, Mexican with Kahlua, Bourbon with Southern Comfort, Russian with Vodka, Normandy with Calvados, or witch's coffee with Strega.

In Ireland and elsewhere the most renowned and recent coffee/alcohol invention, Gaelic (or Irish) coffee, has a world-wide reputation. The merit of the drink was illustrated for me in a restaurant some years ago when an uncle ordered Gaelic coffee for his wife—a lifelong teetotaller—without explaining the contents. On finding that she couldn't have a second one, as it was after hours, my normally demure aunt raised a shriek of protest at the unfortunate waiter who, she imagined, had unreasonably refused to serve her with another coffee. Here is the recipe:

### Gaelic (or Irish) coffee

Heat a stemmed whiskey glass. Pour in a good slug of Irish Whiskey. Add three cubes of sugar. Fill glass with strong black coffee to within one inch of the brim and stir to dissolve sugar. Top to brim of glass with double cream poured carefully over the back of a spoon so that it floats on top of the coffee. Do not stir as the best flavour is obtained by drinking the coffee and Whiskey through the cream.

### Spiced coffee

Spiced coffee is rather a show-off affair, and is flamed in a silver bowl or chafing dish called variously *brule*, *brulot* or *diable*. You need a bowl over a spirit lamp or candle warmer. For 12 to 15 coffee cups, use a bottle of Brandy and $1\frac{1}{2}$ pints of strong coffee. Into the bowl put the thinly pared rind of an orange, 4 large sugar lumps well rubbed with lemon rind to absorb the zest, 4 cloves, an inch of stick cinnamon, an inch of vanilla pod and the Brandy. With a long-handled ladle, lift out some of the warmed Brandy, set it alight and lower it into the bowl to set the mixture alight. Pour in the hot coffee gently, raising the liquid a ladleful at a time to mix everything until the flames die. While the applause for the spectacular display goes on, ladle the mixture into the coffee cups of your appreciative guests.

*Take your coffee straight or laced.*
*Left: Gaelic Coffee crowned with cream.*
*Centre: plunger coffee pot. Right: this shape of cup is known as a 'can'.*

# OF BEER AND CIDER

*An awful lot of ale, beer, lager, stout and what-have-you has been swallowed since William Shakespeare said that 'A quart of ale is a dish for a king'.*

*And come to think of it, an awful lot was poured down before he said it.*

*But why? In theory everything is wrong with beer. Although some 50 billion glasses of the stuff are drunk all over the world each year, hardly anyone actually enjoys his first pint.*

## BEER AND ALE

Beer is quite an acquired taste.

It's cheaper, certainly, than—say—Whisky, but if you take account of the amount of alcohol contained in it, it's just about the most expensive drink in the world. It's 90% water—and who would pay for that? Also, it makes you fat. And it gives you hangovers.

And yet . . . And yet we've been drinking it virtually from time immemorial. We were certainly at it six thousand and more years before Christ was born. Records taken from tombs of that time show recipes for beer. The chances are that it was originally brewed as a kind of offering to the gods who looked after the crops, but some of the congregation discovered that it was much safer to drink than river water, and that it made them feel pretty fit!

Indeed, the Children of Israel are said to have been saved from plague because the alcohol in their beer killed off the germs. Little wonder, then, that the methods of making this particularly delightful medicine spread through the world—although it was not until the sixteenth century that hops were brought into beer-making; before then, barley, wheat, and corn had been used.

The English had been drinking ale, however, for many, many years. Not only drinking it, but making it, for in the days before the traditional tea, every housewife was a brew-it-yourself expert. And, of course, there were the monks who—clever fellows—led the way in the making of many drinks.

Today, England's Burton-on-Trent is renowned for its beer, and has been since the thirteenth century, when the monks in an abbey near Burton found that the local water produced an excellent ale. Modern science shows, in fact, that the water contains various salts, and Burton has remained a brewery centre since the monks' discovery.

In America the first brewery was opened by William Penn in 1683, and gradually science began to make an impression where, previously, results had tended to be somewhat in the lap of the gods. Even so, it wasn't until 1876 that it was really discovered what good beer was all about. Yeast had been used in fermentation before then, but it was in that year that Louis Pasteur found out that wild yeast drifting round a brewery could cause bad fermentation. Yeast, after all, is the key to the whole process, which is otherwise basically rather simple. Briefly, it goes like this:

Processes before fermentation begin with the mixing of different grades of malt (which begins life as barley). The malt is opened by milling to expose enzymes and starches. Other cereals are added, and then the whole thing is mashed in hot water (known to brewers as liquor). The starches are broken down into sugars. Some extra sugar may then be added according to taste, before it is all boiled again—at which point the hops (the female blossoms of the hop vine) are added, to give the familiar bitter flavour. Yeast then ferments the beer. Finally it is cooled and filtered and, hey presto, you've got it. Glorious, clear beer.

Modern science being what it is, boffins have come up with a method of continuous brewing: the four main stages—malting the barley, mashing the malt, boiling the result with hops, and then fermenting with yeast—are done continuously, and the result is that the beer is fermented in a matter of hours rather than weeks.

Ale is made in much the same way as beer, but has a sharper taste and the hop flavour comes through more strongly.

## LAGER

Most of the beer drunk in Britain is what is known as 'draught', whereas most of the world drinks what is generally known in Britain as a lager beer. This first put in an appearance in Germany around the mid-nineteenth century. *Lager* is a German word meaning 'store', which gives some clue to the different taste and colour of the beer. The fermentation process is turned upside-down, as the yeast used, instead of being introduced to the top of the beer, is introduced at the bottom. It takes longer to ferment and requires cold storage—preferably very cold. Caves used to be ideal and the famous Pilsner lager from Czechoslovakia is lagered in six miles of storage caves, dug out of solid limestone. New York was apparently beginning to manufacture its own lager at about the same time as Pilsen. The brewery used a cave which was kept naturally cool by the water from a spring which came to light long after the brewery had moved, when the Eighth Avenue subway was being built, and which led to all kinds of constructional problems.

## STOUT, ETC

Meanwhile, in Ireland they drink pints of *stout*, one after the other! Not only in Ireland now, in fact, because the famous Guinness is drunk almost all over the world. Stout is a dark, heavy ale, often slightly sweet with a taste of malt; its close relative, *porter*, so-called because the London porters used to drink it, is very similar but not quite so strong. Finally, there is *bock*, a special heavy beer, made in the United States from the sediment taken from the fermenting vats during their annual cleaning. It's not to be confused with French bock, which is a glass of light beer.

Throughout history, then, people have been brewing beer. Africans have made it from millet. The Japanese have made it from rice. Europeans, Americans and most other people have made it mainly from barley. But throughout the world, the streamlining and knowledge of both business and scientific techniques have caused complaints in the bar: 'It's not what it used to be'. And, indeed, it may not be. As the large breweries grow bigger and the smaller ones disappear, as the traditional wooden kegs give way to the stainless steel and aluminium barrels, so does the average pint of beer become a little more standardized. At the same time, the chances of being served a beer that is 'off' grow fewer and fewer. So much so, that we can now buy beer in can or bottle, keg or canister, and still have it in superb condition after it's been taken across rough tracks for a picnic on the beach, or carried over heavy seas to be drunk in an English bar on the Champs Elysées.

Some beer is kept well by a landlord —perhaps because of a natural chill in the cellars. Some beer is served badly because pipes are not kept clean. But the

chances of a bad beer leaving the brewery nowadays are virtually nil. As a result, the beer at the King's Head is likely to taste the same as that at the Red Lion or the Queen's Arms. And the lager drunk in South Africa will be pretty much the same as that drunk in Copenhagen.

In consequence, there's very little mystique about beer-drinking. You don't have to know anything about first growths, for the sake of impressing a potential business partner or father-in-law; you don't have to worry unduly about your pocket; you don't have to think about what to drink with the fish. You can simply drift into a bar, virtually anywhere in the world, and say just the two words, 'Beer, please'. Cheers!

## CIDER

People don't usually think of Cider as a wine, and yet, like all wines, it is the fermented juice of a fruit—apples. ('Cider', by the way, comes from 'Shekhar', the Hebrew word for 'strong drink'.) Cider comes in a variety of strengths and forms—still or fizzy, reasonably dry or very sweet. In Britain the main cider producing areas are Herefordshire, Somerset and Devon, and the last two counties are the home of 'scrumpy' which packs a considerable punch. A secondary fermentation may be produced in the bottle by the addition of a small amount of pure cane-sugar syrup, and then the wine is known as 'Champagne' Cider. (In Spain, Cider is always treated in this way.) The result is a delicious basis for wine cups and refreshing summer drinks like:

**Happy apple**
2 parts Calvados
2 parts sparkling Cider
1 dash Angostura
1 level teaspoon caster sugar (dissolved in a little hot water)
1 slice apple
Ice cubes
Stir together in a tumbler. Remove ice, add chilled Cider and drop in apple slice.

## MEAD

Traditionally, a kind of fermented honey. It is sometimes flavoured with herbs, such as cloves, ginger, rosemary hyssop and thyme, when it is known as Metheglin. Mead was quaffed by Ancient Britons and is still regarded by some country people as a cure-all for colds, influenza and hay-fever. It can be light or rich, sweet or dry, still or sparkling.

*In the real English pub, traditional barmaids will still pull you a fine tankard of draught beer.*

49

# LET'S HAVE A PARTY!

*Do it your own way for a relaxed and happy party. There are some general guide-lines, however, and the first is to plan well in advance. That means listing in detail all the things (gadgets and supplies) and also listing all the people you'll want at your party.*

*Give your guests at least two weeks' notice for a 'we're just throwing a party' occasion, a month or so for specific things like weddings, christenings, anniversaries and the like.*

## HOW MANY PEOPLE?

It's a busy world and you can usually reckon that, for special occasions in particular, about five per cent won't be able to come—or will tell you at the last moment that they're sorry. But join the optimists and have the drink and food available for the maximum number. Everyone anyway is more hungry than you think—and there's always someone to help the host finish off the bottle.

## HOW MUCH?

You can generally order your drinks on the sale-or-return basis from most off-licences, paying for all bottles you open and returning the unopened ones. Though the sale-or-return doesn't normally apply at cut-price liquor stores, only at traditional merchants, the cut-price stores may still show you a saving because unopened bottles—of wine, spirits or whatever—won't deteriorate quickly. So you can keep them in a place with an even temperature, somewhere dark and dry, like the larder or under the stairs, for later use. Remember to store table wines on their sides so that their corks stay moist, and don't shrink and let in air. Fortified wines, spirits and beers stand upright.

How much drink do you need for a party? It depends on personal habits and tastes so the better you know your guests' capacities, the more accurately you can judge. Quantities will also vary with the occasion. At hot-weather parties out of doors, people are likely to drink twice as much as they would—say—at a rather more formal dinner party. For this kind of party, where you don't know the capacities of your guests, it's safe to reckon three bottles of table wine for every four people if you're serving only one wine. If you are serving two table wines—a white with the fish, for example, and a red with the main course —allow half a bottle of each wine per head. But in any case, make sure you have some more of the same wine or wines ready, in case they're needed. That means your white wine cool and your reds at the temperature of a warm room (*chambré*). For before and after a meal reckon 12 to 15 drinks from a bottle of Sherry or Port, 8 or 10 from a fine dessert wine like Trockenbeerenauslese or a Sauternes, 6 glasses from a bottle of Champagne, about sixteen glasses from a bottle of made-up aperitif such as Dubonnet, the aniseeds, the bitters or the vermouths. And don't forget that bottles have to be opened— so have a good and reliable corkscrew or two handy and any other opening gadgets that may be needed.

At a buffet party some people tend to drink more freely, others quietly sit on one drink. So it usually averages out much the same.

A tip, if you're serving wine at your buffet, is to arrange the menu so that one wine suits all the food. If there is a second wine it should harmonize pretty generally too, though it could perhaps be slightly sweeter for those who prefer it that way.

## DETAILS THAT COUNT

If the drink is beer, it comes cheaper from most sellers bought in cases of cans than if bought in smaller quantities. Such cans can be handy if fridge space is limited. They stack compactly and you can replenish with new cans as you take cooled ones out. Another way with beer is to buy the 4-pint or 7-pint party size cans. Pouring is quick and easy and the beer stays lively to the end if you fit one of those tap-and-compressor gadgets of the clip-on sort made by Sparklets. Small things like these make pre-planning vital, since you want to be really at home at your own party. Make lists, not only of the obvious things, like the drinks, but of all the equipment and the small garnishes and accompani-ments. A check-list with every item needing attention ticked off is a sure base for the serenity of the party-giver. Citrus fruits (for rind as well as juice), spices like cinnamon, cloves or nutmegs may be included in the drinks you are going to offer. If nutmeg is likely to be one, it's worth getting one of those grinders, like pepper mills, which give a sprinkle of grated nutmeg at the turn of a little wheel or knob. And there are the olives, nuts, cocktail onions, crisps and small biscuits that everyone enjoys nibbling with the drink that welcomes them, whatever the occasion.

## ICE

If there's going to be a big demand for cold drinks and you haven't a hotel-size fridge or ice-maker, you'll need to order ice, either from the fishmonger or an ice supplier. Order that, too, well in advance. At the time when you want it, a lot of other people will be wanting ice too. If necessary—but only if necessary —put any extra ice into the bath (plug-ged) for reserve storage, or keep it out of doors in a cool spot.

## GLASSES

That 'order early' principle applies to glasses, too. Glasses for most occasions, including weddings with Champagne, and for that ancient Brandy after a most important dinner, can well be standard-ized on the ordinary 'tulip' glass. Most of us think of this as 'a wine glass'; it has a short stem and generally holds 5 or 6 ounces of liquid (fluid ounces or simply ounces). The stem allows cool drinks to stay cool while they are drunk but the drinks that flower in warmth can be gently warmed merely by cupping the hand around the bowl of the glass.

But the main point is that the tulip glass in-curves at the rim so that the bouquet, the magic aroma of fine wines and old spirits is concentrated and the sparkle of Champagne, which the makers have spent years of study and hard work to put there, remains to the end of the glass.

So, borrow tulip glasses from your wine merchant when your party is likely to be bigger than your own stock of glasses will meet. Most wine merchants lend them at no charge, except for breakages. But if your party falls at a festive time like Christmas or New Year, do give the poor fellow at least three or four weeks' notice. And if you're borrowing, borrow at least half as many more than the number of your guests. Party people tend to leave partly-finished drinks around; and to run short of glasses to

*An informal, Mediterranean-style party.*

serve the drink in is just as tiresome as running short of the drink to put in them.

## MIXED DRINKS

For most gatherings it helps if the mixed drinks are made in quantity, to be poured from large jugs or ladled from fat-bellied wassail bowls. Punch bowls can sometimes be hired, complete with goblets, but a substitute punch bowl can be one of those Victorian or Edwardian washhand-stand basins or even, American friends say, a pot from the same period which used to go under the bed.

For hot drinks —punches, for instance— you'll add to the style of the party with a fancy ladle (borrowed from friends or bought) rather than a dipping cup. Something else for the list. And for hot drinks, a table-top hot-plate: an electric one or simply a candle-lit one, but a hot-plate that just keeps the drink hot and never boils it.

For cold mixed drinks, chilled ingredients are often better than adding ice in the glass. Use plenty of ice to cool the bottles and other ingredients. So perhaps add a couple of kitchen buckets to the list. Or you can cover those you already have with aluminium foil. Special ways of using ice are discussed in the sections on soft drinks and summer coolers. Another thing which can be done in advance is the preparation of sugar syrup, a useful stand-by for lots of sweetening jobs; a recipe for it is given on page 57.

## MAKING SPACE

Something else for the list are ways of making room for your guests. What may be a spacious home on normal occasions can be like a bus in the rush hour when you bring 30 to 40 of your friends into it. So pack away the ornaments, the television set, and indeed anything which won't serve a purpose as putting-down space or sitting-down space. A lot of people enjoy standing to chat and drink but others like to sit. For one of the best summer buffets we ever gave, for about 50 guests, we arranged with some of our close friends to bring along their collapsible garden and picnic chairs and cushions. One item not to be removed, of course—the ashtrays. Indeed you increase them, so that they are easy to find everywhere.

## THE INVALUABLE CHECK-LIST

Here is a list of the items you might need, and of things to be done: you can build your own list from it:
Number of guests asked
Number of guests expected

(Useful to make a note if there is something which one of your guests can't eat or drink)
Drinks:
  What you are going to serve
  Number of bottles needed
  (Remember that you'll need a number of bottles in reserve)
Glasses:
  Your own
  Borrowed
Extra ice
Ice buckets or a substitute
Foil to line the substitute buckets
Corkscrew(s) and other openers
Tap and compressor attachment for large beer or cider cans
Items for mixed drinks:
  Citrus fruits
  Nutmeg (and nutmeg grinder)
  Other spices
  Sugar syrup
  Large jug or bowl
  Ladle (or dipping cup)
Table-top hot-plate for hot drinks
Ashtrays (and matches)
Food titbits:
  Olives
  Cocktail onions
  Nuts
  Crisps
  Savoury biscuits
Extra furniture needed (if any)
Any necessary cutlery
Plates
Napkins

## WEDDINGS AND OTHER OCCASIONS

Weddings, christenings, birthdays, anniversaries, and perhaps most of all, wakes, are emotional occasions. They are times for happiness, or reverence, or a mixture of many feelings.

A little know-how and some advance planning before the day arrives will help to make things go calmly and well, as far as the practical side—the organization of the catering—is concerned. Indeed, forethought can make all these events into simple occasions, basically no different from the times when you invite friends to a meal. So, many of the thoughts about general entertaining apply here, too. They're worth looking at carefully, since they cover a list of quantities of food and drink for all sorts of times when you have more than your family to cater for.

Let us be specific about the wedding first, although the things to be said can apply to other gatherings, too. You decide, first, whether the reception will be at a local hotel or restaurant or whether you'll run it yourself at home— a decision which will depend on what the local public facilities are as well as on

how many friends, relations and other helpers you can mobilise for a home 'do' One good reason for choosing a local hotel or restaurant is that the people there are accustomed to dealing with large numbers of guests. Before you make up your mind, it's worth talking to them. If you like their food, ask the prices of the various menus they can provide for the number of guests you will have.

If you decide on a meal, it should be cheaper, because of the numbers, than anything similar composed from their regular menu, even allowing for the inclusion of extras suitable to the special occasion. Consult the manager or the catering manager about that and about the wines and their prices. Many hotels can offer a choice of menus at all-in prices, sometimes including a sherry for guests as they arrive. If not, you'll have to do your own sums from the wine list. Which wines? If the reception involves sitting down to a hotel meal, harmonize the wine with the courses—a white and a red probably. Or you can choose a wine to go right through the meal. Champagne, some say, goes right through a meal but it's better to have a dry one as an aperitif and a fuller-bodied one with the food. Another way is to serve Champagne for just the major toast (the bride and groom, or whatever is appropriate to the occasion) and simple red or white table wine with the food.

These guide lines apply equally if you stage the gathering—wedding, christening or birthday—at home. The main alternative is a buffet rather than a sit-down reception. Here you can offer with the various foods, to which the guests will help themselves, comparatively modest wines (white, rosé or red according to the foods). It's a good idea, too, to have, as an alternative to wine, a good summer cup or a cold punch. It helps the party spirit no end.

Another idea, in hotel or home, is to serve coffee. It can signal the approaching end of the party, sometimes hard to indicate otherwise. But it doesn't have to be dull. Lace the coffee, making sure that the coffee is strong, really strong, to begin with (see the section on coffee page 46).

### Royal Fizz

This Champagne Special for the main toast is especially fortifying, since it contains an egg per person.

For each guest allow a double Brandy, 1 egg, juice of 1 lemon and 1 tablespoonful sugar syrup. Mix all ingredients except the Brandy in the blender, strain and stir in the Brandy well.

Pour a little into wine glasses, add an ice cube and top up with Champagne.

# DIPS AND DUNKS

*Pretty presentation is essential—vegetables must be as crisp, and fresh as possible, while biscuits should be spread at the last minute so that they don't become soggy.*

## DIPS

Here are a few suggestions for things to serve with dips: Potato crisps, Indian popadoms, prawn crackers, small savoury biscuits, Gristicks, cooked shrimps, frankfurter chunks, or cocktail sausages, raw vegetables like sticks of celery, carrots, radishes, spring onions, French bread or baked croutons.

**SOUR CREAM DIP** (serves 6)
**5 oz. carton of soured cream**
**1 tablespoon of chilli sauce**
**(from a bottle)**
**1 teaspoon of dried mustard powder**
**1 medium onion (grated)**
**1 teaspoon of Worcester sauce**
**1 tablespoon of snipped chives**
**½ teaspoon freshly-ground pepper**
**½ teaspoon of salt**
Mix everything together, and chill one hour before serving.

**AVOCADO DIP** (serves 6)
**1 medium-sized ripe avocado**
**1 tablespoon of lemon juice**
**5 oz. carton of soured cream**
**1 clove of garlic (crushed)**
**1 medium onion (grated)**
**Half a green pepper (chopped small)**
**Salt, freshly-ground black pepper**
**2 tomatoes (chopped small)**
1. Slice the avocado in two and remove the stone.
2. Scoop out all the pulp into a bowl, making sure you get all the very green flesh next to the skin (this helps to make the dip a good colour).
3. Thoroughly mix in the tablespoon of lemon juice, the salt and freshly-milled black pepper.

*Top: Sour Cream Dip served with crunchy pieces of carrot and cauliflower to scoop it up with. Centre: biscuits with a variety of savoury spreads. Below: Savoury Cheese Straws (see overleaf ). All are shown served on a handsome endgrain teak board.*

53

4. Now add the soured cream and mix till smooth, either with rotary whisk or electric beater.
5. Add the garlic, onion, green pepper and tomatoes. Stir, taste to check the seasoning and chill before serving. Never make this until the day you need it, as it tends to discolour if left overnight.

### BLUE CHEESE DIP (serves 6)
**¼ lb. of gorgonzola cheese**
**5 oz. carton of soured cream**
**1 medium onion (grated)**
**1 teaspoon of freshly-ground pepper**
1. Cream the cheese by mixing with a large fork.
2. Add the soured cream, a little at a time, until it's all in and the mixture looks creamy.
3. Add the grated onion and pepper.
4. Chill in the refrigerator.

## SAVOURIES FOR SPREADING ON BISCUITS

### KIPPER PATÉ (serves 6)
**1 10 oz. packet of frozen kipper fillets**
**1 small onion (chopped very small)**
**4 oz. butter (room temperature)**
**The juice of a medium lemon**
**¼ whole nutmeg**
**Salt, pepper, paprika**
1. Cook the kipper fillets according to the instructions on the pack, drain and allow to cool.
2. Remove the skins and put the fillets into a mixing-bowl. Mash to a pulp with a large fork.
3. Add onions, lemon juice and butter, and mash again with the fork until all is smooth and creamy.
4. Add grated nutmeg, and season to taste with salt and pepper.
5. Chill for one hour.
6. Spread paté on small biscuits, sprinkle with paprika and decorate with slices of stuffed olive or gherkin.

### CHEESE AND PEPPER SPREAD (serves 6)
**1 lb. of cheddar cheese (grated)**
**6 spring onions (chopped very small)**
**1 small red pepper (seeded and chopped small)**
**4 oz. of mayonnaise**
1. Put all the ingredients into a large mixing-bowl and blend evenly.
2. Serve spread on small biscuits.

### QUICK PATÉ (serves 6)
**2 rashers of bacon**
**Cooking oil**
**18 oz. can of paté**
**1 clove of garlic (crushed)**
**¼ teaspoon of dried mixed herbs**
**Freshly-milled black pepper**
**1 tablespoon of Brandy**
**A few gherkins (sliced)**
**Some slices of tomato**
1. Fry the bacon in oil till crisp and well-done. Drain on kitchen paper.
2. Chop bacon finely.
3. Mix bacon, paté, garlic and herbs, and Brandy. Season with freshly-milled black pepper and salt.
4. Chill, and serve on small biscuits with slices of gherkin or tomato on top.

### SHRIMP PATÉ (serves 6)
**½ lb. of peeled prawns (thawed if frozen)**
**4 teaspoons of olive oil**
**The juice of a small lemon**
**A few gratings of nutmeg**
**Salt, and a pinch of cayenne pepper**
**2 oz. of peeled prawns for garnish**
**A little paprika**
1. Put the prawns, olive oil, lemon juice and nutmeg into the goblet of a liquidizer and blend till you have a smooth paste.
2. Empty into a bowl and season with salt and cayenne, according to taste.
3. Chill.
4. Serve spread on savoury biscuits and garnish with whole prawns and a sprinkling of paprika.

## SAVOURIES ON STICKS

1. Melon cubes, wrapped in thin strips of Parma Ham.
2. Chopped celery stalks, stuffed with a mixture of cream cheese and chopped walnuts.
3. Fresh pineapple cubes with slices of Swiss Gruyère cheese.
4. Small chunks of Spanish chorizo sausage.
5. Cubes of garlic sausage spiked with slices of pickled pimento.

### SAVOURY CHEESE STRAWS
**8 oz. of plain flour**
**Salt and cayenne pepper**
**4 oz. of butter**
**3 oz. of strong cheddar cheese (grated)**
**1 oz. of grated parmesan**
**2 egg yolks**
**Cold water**
Heat oven to 400 °F (Gas Mark 6, 200 °C).
1. Put flour into a mixing-bowl, with a little salt and cayenne pepper.
2. Rub in butter until the mixture resembles fine breadcrumbs.
3. Mix in grated cheeses thoroughly.
4. Add beaten egg yolks and enough cold water to make a stiff dough.
5. Turn out onto a floured board and roll out pastry into an oblong about 15 inches long and 5 inches wide.
6. Cut into straws approximately 2½ inches long and ¼ inch wide.
7. Twist each straw and place them on a prepared greased baking-tray.
8. Bake for 10-15 minutes until golden-brown. Cool and store in an airtight tin. This mixture can also be used to make small cheese biscuits.

# HOT'N PUNCHY

*Breaking the ice can have more than a social meaning. There are those days and nights when frost and snow make a hot drink the best welcome and the best stirrup-cup for the departing guest.*

## SOUP – LACED OR PLAIN

If it's an eats-and-drinks party, a light soup to stimulate the appetite, rather than cloy it. A home-made beef tea, a clear chicken broth or a consommé go well. They go even better if the beef tea is laced with Whisky (or pretty well any other clear spirit, to your taste), and you can give clear soups an air of sophistication with a touch of dry Sherry from Spain, one of the variants from Cyprus, Australia or South Africa, or a Sercial from Madeira. Whatever you use, it needs only about a tablespoonful added to each bowl or cup, just before serving.

## MULLS, TODDIES AND OTHERS

There's a long list of party drinks that can be hot. Punches, possets, mulls, toddies and grogs—all good warmer-uppers, even their names sing a happy party song. And, besides providing fun in the making as well as in the drinking, they can be comparatively easy on the purse. Obviously since they are mixed drinks, deriving their character from sugar, spices and other non-wine ingredients, it would be folly to use fine wines for them. Where a recipe says Claret or Burgundy, any of the most bourgeois growths will be quite satisfactory—or, indeed, any wine of similar style from another country, whether it is a branded wine or not.
But do try them out first. For that matter, since most of these drinks specify sugar, spices and other ingredients 'to taste', they're all worthy of a little rehearsal before the party—say, with your family or a few friends. It isn't a painful exercise. Another important point is that since the drinks are hot, they're best served in goblets or other containers which have handles. Silver or pewter may be considered status

*For a large party, big bowls of punch or wine cup are easier to cope with than lots of different drinks.*

symbols but, in fact, metal cups conduct heat and may be a hazard to tender lips, so little china or glass mugs are better. If they're glass and your toddy is really hot —which is the object of the exercise—a spoon placed in the cup during the pouring will dissipate the heat and save breakages.

One other point: mulls, punches and the like used to be warmed by plunging a red-hot poker in them. Nowadays it's much more efficient to heat them gently on the stove. Get them hot but never let them boil unless you want to drive off all the benign influence of the alcohol —which you don't, presumably, or you wouldn't be reading this.

## PUNCHES

Let's take punches, for instance. In the eighteenth century the making of punch was a high-society ritual, undertaken with flourish and solemnity. The bewigged host, standing at the head of his table, had the undivided attention of his guests as they watched him summon servant after servant to bring each successive ingredient to go into the punch bowl.

Punch is still fun. To begin with, it's a natural starter for general conversation. Does the word 'punch' come from the Hindustani *panch* (meaning five), since the ingredients when it was first introduced from India in the seventeenth century were five—spirit, fruit juice, water, spices and sugar? But weren't some of those original recipes of only three ingredients and some of them of six ingredients? And anyhow, isn't it simpler to take the word simply to be an abbreviation of 'puncheon', the name of the casks from which the sailors on the East India run drew their grog rations? "But," says your favourite extrovert guest, "does all this matter—when your punch is the greatest?" If he is being truthful, the heart of your successful punch will still be those five ingredients, though the proportions can be infinitely varied, according to your guests, to their tastes and capacities—and to yours too. As to quantities for a party, a couple of ¼-pint punch goblets are enough for some, too much for others. It is up to you to know the inexperienced drinkers, who can be quietly given a bit more hot water and fruit juice, and the rather more experienced ones, who take your standard-mixture punch. Again, it's worth some rehearsal. Here's a warmer-upper which truly began in the eighteenth century and is sometimes called Dr. Johnson's Choice. It makes about 12 to 15 punch glasses or goblets.

### Dr. Johnson
Heat two bottles of Claret gently with one sliced orange, 12 lumps of sugar which have been rubbed on the orange rind, and six cloves. Bring the mixture nearly to the boil and remove it from the stove, immediately adding a wineglassful (say, 6 fl. oz.) of one of the orange liqueurs (branded Cointreau, Grand Marnier, South Africa's Van der Hum or simply Curaçao) and the same quantity of Brandy. Ladle it into your punch cups and sprinkle each with nutmeg.

### The Bishop
For 12 to 15 drinks, stud a lemon with cloves and bake it in a moderate oven for 30 minutes. Heat 2 pints of Port to just below simmering point. In another pan boil 1 pint water with 1 teaspoonful mixed spices and add it to the hot Port with the baked lemon. Rub 2 oz. lump sugar into the rind of another lemon and put this sugar into the punch bowl with the juice of ½ lemon and pour in the hot wine.

## MULLS

Mulls are basically sugared and spiced wines, beers or ciders, very like punches and served, if you choose, with the same ceremoniousness. They are usually diluted with water, served really hot, but laced with fortified wines, spirits or liqueur, added after the heating. One which also has the Dickensian name of Negus is:

### Red Wine Mull
For 8 drinks, boil a pint of water with 2 tablespoonsful of sugar, 10 cloves, some slices of lemon and grated nutmeg. Warm a bottle of red table wine in a pan, remove it from the heat and stir in the spiced boiling water. Add 2 to 6 fl. oz. of Brandy or other spirit—kind and quantity to your taste—and serve at once.

### White Wine Mull
For 10 to 12 drinks, gently heat 2 bottles of dry white wine with the juice of 2 lemons and six tablespoonsful of honey (your choice of honey since it comes in all sorts of flavours). Before pouring the mixture into the goblets, add ½ pint of Brandy, White Rum, Vodka, the Scandinavian Aquavit or other spirit.

### Lamb's Wool
To make 10 to 12 drinks of this beer mull, which takes its name from the frothy sieved apple in it, bake 8 or 10 clove-studded cooking apples in the oven. Mash them with 2 to 2½ pints of old ale (or draught brown ale) and add, to taste, ground ginger, nutmeg and sugar. Heat the mixture gently, without boiling, and serve it hot.

## POSSETS

Possets, which used to be popular, particularly as Christmas drinks, began as health drinks, cures for colds and other ailments. But they became popular party drinks: Samuel Pepys records that he sent his guests away 'highly pleased' after a posset. Fundamentally they are mulls made with milk or eggs, or both, curdled by ale or wine. A traditional one is called Huckle-my-Buff, said to be old Sussex slang and impossible to translate!

### Huckle-my-Buff
For 12 drinks, beat a dozen eggs thoroughly with 2 pints of draught beer and ¼ lb. sugar. Heat the mixture but take it off the heat before it boils. Add another 2 pints of beer, 4 teaspoonsful of grated nutmeg and Brandy or other spirit to taste.

### Auld Man's Milk
Another posset is Auld Man's Milk, basically Scots and so made with Whisky, but equally happily made with Rum, Vodka, Aquavit or any other spirit. To make a dozen drinks separate a dozen eggs, beat the yolks well with ¾ lb. sugar and then beat this mixture into 3 pints of milk and 1 pint of Whisky, with a teaspoonful of ground cinnamon. Warm the mixture. Whisk the egg whites thoroughly and fold them into the warm mixture, again thoroughly.

### Yard of Flannel
Yet another posset, called Yard of

**Hot Tea Punch**
Take ½ pint each of Jamaica Rum and Brandy and pour into a warmed metal bowl. Add juice of one lemon, and set alight. Add 2 pints hot, strong, strained tea in which ½ lb powdered sugar has been dissolved.

Flannel, can form a dramatic climax to any party but—be earnestly warned—it needs plenty of practice by the host or it is in danger of becoming a terribly messy anti-climax.

For 8 drinks you need 3 pints of strong ale, 8 eggs, $\frac{1}{4}$ lb. sugar, $\frac{1}{2}$ pint Rum, 2 teaspoonsful of ground ginger. Warm the ale. Beat thoroughly together the eggs, sugar, Rum and ginger and put the mixture into a large jug. When the ale is nearly boiling pour it into another jug and pour from one jug to the other until the mixture is quite smooth. Pouring swiftly with ever-expanding distance between the jugs can be a triumph of skill but—remember! remember!—it does need practice.

## Hot Egg Nog

For every two drinks, beat one whole egg and one yolk with 1 tablespoonful of sugar and 2 tablespoonsful Whisky. Add, beating vigorously, $\frac{3}{4}$ pint of hot (not boiling) milk. As variations, the amount of Whisky can be doubled or even trebled and instead of Whisky you can use any spirit or liqueur or double the quantity of Marsala, Madeira, Port or Sherry.

## HOT TODDIES AND GROGS

Making these by the glass, put into each goblet 2 oz. Rum, 1 oz. concentrated orange juice (straight from the can), 1 teaspoonful caster sugar and 2 cloves. Top up with hot water, stir and give each goblet an orange-slice float and a sprinkle of grated nutmeg. As a variation, use lemon juice instead of orange, fill up with hot freshly brewed tea (strained) and garnish with a twist of lemon rind.

## ALE AND CIDER

Cold-night comforters can be made with ale or cider as tastes (and maybe budgets) dictate.

### Spiced Ale

Heat mild rather than heavily hopped beer with grated nutmeg or ground cinnamon and brown sugar, all to taste, plus a twist of lemon rind. The addition afterwards of a measure of Brandy or other spirit is optional.

### Golden Cider Mull

For 6 drinks, put $\frac{1}{4}$ pint of water in a small saucepan with 12 cloves, a 3-inch cinnamon stick, 3 blades of mace, a little grated nutmeg, $1\frac{1}{2}$ oz. brown sugar, 1 lemon and 1 orange. Bring to the boil and simmer gently for 15 minutes. Meantime, stud 4 small oranges with cloves and bake them in a moderate oven for 15 minutes. Add the boiled spice mixture to 3 pints of still cider and reheat before straining it into the punch bowl. Add the baked oranges to float in the bowl.

# LONG & COOL FOR SUMMER

*Wine cups make excellent summer thirst-quenchers. They're delicious laced with liqueurs or with spirits, and are often a welcome variation at weddings and other festive occasions, or for picnics and lunches, or supper in a summer garden. Served from glass jugs or bowls, they look good, too, if decorated attractively—so long as they're not served as fruit salad in disguise! The simpler and the subtler, the better.*

## ICE

Ice makes all the difference to so many drinks. Some recipes call for crushed ice. It's possible to crush ice cubes in some electric blenders, but chill the goblet first, and look at the instructions with your particular blender, to see if it can be used for this. Otherwise use the traditional method: wrap ice cubes in a teacloth and then in a folded towel, and then hammer like mad—with a hammer or mallet.

Ice cubes can look decorative, too. Boil the water first and let it get cold, then the final cubes will be that much clearer. You can use small strawberries or raspberries, cocktail cherries, red or blackcurrants, a tiny sprig of mint, a little piece of orange or lemon flesh—all these separately, of course—to put in each cube section of the ice trays. Add the cold boiled water to the tray (or trays) and freeze. When you come to serve individual drinks or generous bowls of cool punch, the garnish in the cubes will show up attractively.

## WINES TO USE

Wine cups don't need expensive wines. The most modest suit them well and, indeed, it would be ostentatious to use fine wines in these mixed drinks. Where a recipe mentions Claret or Burgundy, or a white Rhine wine or Moselle, any similar style of wine will do just as well. Equally, in a Champagne cup, use non-vintage Champagne or you have a wide choice of many bubbly wines, made by the Champagne method or the less expensive *cuve close*. Besides Spanish sparkling and the German *sekts* (sparkling Hocks or Moselle), there is sparkling Vouvray, sparkling Saumur, Asti Spumante, and many others. They will all show a substantial saving in the party budget, and so will sparkling Cider and, indeed, soda-water made by your own Sparklets system.

Wine cups are also very adaptable.

Without any obvious difference in their appearance, they can be only mildly alcoholic for youngsters or strengthened effectively with an extra lacing of spirits or liqueurs.

## FRUIT FOR SUMMER COOLERS

In cups, as in all mixed drinks where lemon or orange rind is listed, it doesn't mean the whole peel, but only the yellow (or orange) part. Using a sharp knife pare it as thinly as possible off the white pith.

## SUGAR SYRUP

Put 1 lb. of sugar and 1 pint of water in a saucepan. Dissolve over gentle heat. Bring to boil and boil to 104°C (220°F). Cool and bottle for future use.

## HERBS

Fresh herbs will add dash to your wine cups, too. Borage, lemon mint, balm, sweet verbena and bergamot are some of the less common ones to get.

All the ingredients of cold cups, cold punches and the like should be well chilled (but not frozen) before they go into your mixture. If you are adding ice, you will keep the original balance of the cup better by adding large chunks rather than small ice cubes. Take out the separators from the ice trays in your fridge, and you will get handy-sized blocks for breaking up. But chill everything as well.

Soda-water or other bubbly drinks should be added to cups at the last minute. If at this stage the drink seems not sweet enough, add sugar syrup or liqueur. Above there is a recipe for sugar syrup to keep in stock; it's much better than sugar itself for adjusting the sweetness of cold cups). If your wine cup seems too sweet, then a glass of dry Sherry will sharpen it. And give the glass jug or bowl a deep stir from time to time, so that all the ingredients remain evenly mixed.

# RECIPES

### Vermouth Cassis
1 measure of Cassis syrup, 2 of dry Vermouth, topped up with soda-water. Any other fruit syrup can be used—*grenadine* (pomegranate) or *fraise* (strawberry), for example. And if you like it stronger, use a liqueur instead of a syrup.

### Pimm's
This is one of England's great traditional drinks. It says Henley and Ascot and Goodwood and Glyndebourne, and garden parties and tennis—in fact, it says all the good things about summer days out of doors in the sunshine. Pimm's is a simple drink. It's too often abused by people putting half the fruit and vegetable garden into it, as well as too much ice and lemonade and little plastic umbrellas! The recipe on the Pimm's bottle should be followed exactly: 3 to 4 parts of ice-cold lemonade to 1 part of Pimm's No. 1 (Gin based), add a sliver of cucumber and a slice of lemon and serve in silver tankards or ½-pint mugs.
For a drier version, replace some of the lemonade with soda-water or a shot of Vodka or Gin. For a sweeter drink, add a shot of Curaçao or Cherry Brandy. And you can ring other changes with bottled aperitifs like St. Raphael, Byrrh or Dubonnet, or with straight spirits. Another idea is to make a Pimm's Royale, using Champagne instead of lemonade. A 'Pimola' is Pimm's with Coca Cola, and it's excellent if the Coca Cola is ice-cold and a slice of fresh lime is added to cut down the sweetness. Pimm's made with fresh orange juice is reputed to be the 'in thing' in Australia (is it called a Pimgaroo?).
The formula for Pimm's is a secret known only to the managing director; employees of the firm have to sign a kind of 'Official Secrets Act' document when they join. Basically, the drink is a blend of high-quality Gin, herbs and liqueurs, and it dates back to 1814 and today it is available in every country in the world.

### Perrier Plus
Chilled Perrier (or other gassy spring water) makes a good dilutant for most spirits. A simple fruit cup is 2 measures Gin, 1 measure fresh lime juice, topped up with Perrier and a slice of lime.

### Black Velvet
A half-and-half mixture of Champagne and Guinness, both well chilled, and fashionably served in silver goblets.

### Buck's Fizz
A half-and-half mixture of Champagne and fresh orange juice, both well chilled. Many people reckon that this is a waste of Champagne, and use sparkling wine.

### Rothschild
Make a strawberry crush (recipe on page 64), and put it with crushed ice into long glasses. Top them up with Champagne (you'll need 1 bottle to make between 10 and 12 glasses). Serve immediately.

### Mint Julep
Put 10 or 12 tender shoots of young mint with sugar to taste in a tumbler and bruise the mint slightly with a spoon. Add Bourbon or a half-and-half mixture of Bourbon and liqueur, until the tumbler is anything from a quarter to a half full. Then fill it up with crushed ice and drink as the ice melts. This is not unlike the iced liqueurs which the French call *frappé*—like Crème de Menthe poured over crushed ice.

### Wine Juleps
Put young mint sprigs in a tumbler or wine glass, with sugar to taste, and crush slightly. Then fill up with the wine of your choice—rosé or white, sparkling or still.

### Wine cups
The standard method is to put a block of ice in a jug, add 2 measures each of two liqueurs—say, Curaçao and Maraschino, or Bénédictine and Chartreuse—and pour in two bottles of any still wine or still Cider. You can get colour variations by your choice of wines and liqueurs: for instance, a delightful pink wine cup comes from using a red liqueur with a rosé wine, or a mixture of rosé and white. And you can tinge white wines with a proportion of ruby Port.
That old Port-and-lemon—ruby Port topped up with fizzy lemonade—is still a good mixture for those who like sweet things. A chilled white Port topped up with chilled soda-water is a drier summer cooler; it's popular (and socially acceptable) in Portugal.

### Hock Sparkler
For 20 to 25 drinks, chill 2 bottles of Hock, 1 bottle of sparkling Hock, 1 glass of Brandy, ½ lb. of skinned seedless grapes and sugar syrup. Mix the still Hock and the grapes, sweeten to taste, and leave them in the fridge for an hour. Add the sparkling Hock and serve, decorated with chilled chopped peaches.

### Planters' Punch
For 15 to 18 drinks, dissolve 2 lbs. of sugar in ½ pint of fresh lemon juice, and chill well. Chill also ½ pint of dark Rum, ½ pint of Brandy, 3 pints of water, and your mixing bowl or jug. Put a good chunk of ice in the bowl and pour everything over it. Then you can top each glass with a grating of nutmeg or a slice of lime, or both.

### Safari Punch
For 20 glasses, chill and mix 1 bottle of sweet or medium sweet white wine, 1

pint of draught Cider, ¼ bottle of Brandy and the same amount of passion fruit juice. Chill also 1 lemon, 1 orange and 1 cored apple. Slice lemon and orange and cut apple (still with its skin on) into segments and put them in the bowl as a float. Just before serving add a bottle of chilled fizzy lemonade.

### Fish House Punch
One of the most publicized of punches, said to have originated in the Philadelphia Club in 1732; there are a dozen or more recipes claiming to be authentic. It's good and potent, and this recipe is at least close to the original, although that specified fresh spring water. It makes enough for about 25 people, allowing about ½ pint each. It takes 2 bottles of Rum (dry or dark to taste), 1 bottle of Brandy, 1¼ pints of lemon juice (it must be fresh lemon juice), 2½ pints of water, ½ pint of sugar syrup. Some versions of the recipe specify ¼ pint of Peach Brandy (Peach *Eau de Vie* in Europe). Others specify the sweeter peach liqueur, and if you use that, you may decide that you need less sugar syrup.

### Fiesta Punch
For 12 drinks, mix 1 bottle of sweet white wine, ½ pint of sugar syrup, juice of 1 lemon, 1 can unsweetened pineapple juice. Add ice, slices of orange and cubes of melon and, finally, a bottle of chilled soda-water.

### Sangria
A Spanish potion which has spread. For 15, marinate in 2 good measures of Brandy slices of apple, pear, orange and lemon for 30 minutes. Put a block of ice in the bowl, add 1 bottle of red wine, 2 measures of Brandy, slices of marinated fruit and/or berries, and finally 1 bottle of chilled fizzy lemonade.

### Sangaree
Possibly a corruption of *Sangria*. For an Ale Sangaree, a tablespoonful of sugar syrup per tumbler, filled up with ale (or other beer), and dusted with grated nutmeg.
Wine Sangarees are made with less or more sugar syrup, according to the table wine you use; those made with sweet fortified wine (1 wine glass to each tumbler) need no sweetening, and are topped up with iced water.
Whisky Sangaree follows the same method as Ale Sangaree, using a few ice cubes instead of the ale.
Sangarees can be hot for winter.

*Summer punches can be based on wine, rum, brandy, whisky or even ale.*
*Left: a luscious jug of Safari Punch, decorated and flavoured with slices of apple and orange. Above right: summer coolers look best when decoration is kept within bounds.*

## WINE AND CHEESE PARTIES

Among buffets a wine and cheese party is among the easiest, and also the most economical. Apart from getting the house ready, you need to make minimum preparation. Allow about 4 to 6 ounces of cheese per person, a bit more for a cheese that may prove to be the favourite. It's simplest to limit the number of cheeses, so that they can be in sizeable lumps, or—even better—whole cheeses. If you can be sure of getting Brie or Camembert at the peak of maturity, get a whole one, or two (or more) according to the size of the party. Safer perhaps are the pressed cheeses which keep well: Stilton, Wensleydale, Double Gloucester, Cheshire, Cheddar and Caerphilly, Holland's Edam and Gouda, France's goat-milk cheese like Chabichou and Chavignol, Italy's Bel Paese, Switzerland's Gruyère and Emmenthal.

Try to offer different styles of cheeses. Have the milder ones at the starting-point of your buffet table, where your guests pick up plate, knife and napkin. Work up to the fruitiest at the other end—say a Roquefort, a Gorgonzola, a Danish Blue or a ripe Stilton. Fresh French loaves, which your guests cut themselves, or unsweetened biscuits are ideal accompaniments. Butter is optional but usually appreciated.

Keep the wines simple too—a dry or medium dry white to go with the milder cheeses, fuller-bodied reds for the more flavourful. The ultimate refinement is to offer a wine from the same region as the cheese—a rich Rhône to accompany Roquefort, for instance, or a Chianti Classico or a Barbaresco with the Gorgonzola. But Burgundies, Clarets and Chinon from the Loire are recognized as classic accompaniments to cheese, too, and by long tradition Port is the ideal partner to Stilton.

Obviously, a cheese and wine party is at its most effective when numbers are large. You can make it a bit more elaborate by serving a fondu, dip or *quiche*.

### Cheese dip

A simple dip can be made by blending ¾ lb. cream cheese with 5 oz. of sour cream, laced with 4 oz. bacon, crisply grilled and broken up into tiny pieces. Make it early in the day and serve it cold with crisp vegetable dunkers, also prepared early and kept fresh in water or try one of the other dips on page 53. And a couple of attractive asparagus *quiches*, incorporating grated Cheddar in the crust and grated Parmesan in the cream-and-eggs filling, can be made the day before and reheated in the oven at 400°F (Gas Mark 6, 200°C) for 15 minutes.

Even the wisest of us sometimes wish we hadn't had quite so many, or such varied, drinks the night before.

## What causes hang-overs?
Quite simply, hang-overs are caused by Too Much. Of course, one man's excess may be another's aperitif, and even your own vulnerability may vary from day to day, depending on how well or tired you are, and whether the poor system is being strained in some other way – through over-eating or too much smoking. Basically it's a kind of poisoning – the system gets flooded with alcohol and can't get rid of it quickly enough. The question is, are there any real remedies for this lugubrious condition?

## Food before
It's always wise to eat well before spending an evening drinking rather than eating. It gives the lining of the stomach a buffer against the onslaught of alcohol.

## Dangerous drinks
Some drinks are more likely to produce a hang-over in some people than others – for example, red wine, rum, whisky and, most lethal of all, brandy. On the other hand, you're more likely to wake up feeling fresh and happy after drinking white wine, gin or vodka. The operative word is OR. Mixing wines and spirits is liable to lead to trouble too. Beware also of too much cheap champagne, cheap sour wine, and unidentified fruit cups!

## Water
The best answer of course, is to drink lots and lots of water on getting home from the party and before going to bed, with or without some fizzy additive. Two pints of water will do more for the pain than anything else as alcohol is very dehydrating and the dehydration is a prime cause of headaches. If you forgot to drink a lot of water just before you went to bed, drink much more water than you feel you actually want when you wake.

## Cigarettes
Half the trouble with many parties is the quantity of smoke which creates a heavy, thick atmosphere guaranteed to produce headaches. Cigarette smoking aggravates the effects of drinking too.

# AFTER THE PARTY'S OVER...

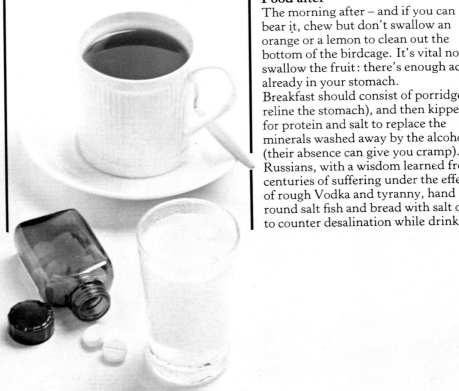

## Kaolin and Morphine mixture
If someone is feeling distinctly queasy, he should pop into a chemist and down a dose of Kaolin and Morphine mixture. It settle the stomach miraculously and stops the boat rocking.

## Patent Cures
Fernet Branca is an Italian bitters which certainly lives up to that description. Perhaps it's the shock of the flavour or the soothing properties of the herbs but either way, some people find it curative. Underberg is a German cure – very alcoholic and very effective.

## Curative recipes
These are really designed for people who are longing for a reviving sip of alcohol but realise it should be tempered with a good, nutritional base. Prairie Oyster is a mixture of 1 oz brandy, 1 teasp. wine vinegar, 1 teasp. Worcester sauce, a dash Cayenne pepper and 1 egg yolk.
Pour the first four ingredients over the egg and swallow – if possible – without breaking the egg!
Both a Bloody Mary and a Bull Shot (see Cocktails section) give a good cushion of tomato juice or consommé.

## Oxygen
Medical students swear by a whiff of oxygen. A few deep breathes at an open window or a brisk walk are helpful for anyone without a cylinder to hand. Some sufferers find that in mountainous country a journey up the ski-lift above 5,000 feet will work wonders.

## Food after
The morning after – and if you can bear it, chew but don't swallow an orange or a lemon to clean out the bottom of the birdcage. It's vital not to swallow the fruit: there's enough acid already in your stomach.
Breakfast should consist of porridge (to reline the stomach), and then kippers, for protein and salt to replace the minerals washed away by the alcohol (their absence can give you cramp). The Russians, with a wisdom learned from centuries of suffering under the effects of rough Vodka and tyranny, hand round salt fish and bread with salt on it to counter desalination while drinking.

# CHOOSING GLASS

*The first requirement of a modern glass is that one should be able to see through it in order to enjoy the colour of the liquid. This rules out ruby-bowled hock glasses and the heavily decorated variety.*

Bertrand Russell, at the close of a stormy life that had included gaol sentences, divorces, and active support for the pacifist cause, said that the only moment of stark terror he could remember was when he was a boy of 17; at the end of dinner the ladies retired, leaving him alone with Mr. Gladstone, the Liberal Prime Minister, who directed the full force of his indignation at poor young

Russell, because he had been given Port in a Claret glass! It is a well-known fault of the British that they take the outward form of things too seriously, but I doubt if anyone would care now as much as Mr. Gladstone did.

## BASIC EQUIPMENT

Glass is not a problem, nor need it be much of an expense. The following four shapes will do for all drinks without causing a raised eyebrow among your guests:

**Basic stemmed glass** with rounded Paris (15) or tulip-shaped (3) bowl for red or white wine. The 8 oz. size is best; a 12 oz. light-ale goblet will either run you out of drink too soon, or knock your friends out too early.

**Old fashioned:** (4) a short, wide tumbler modelled on the heavy-based Whisky glass (10). It does for punch as well as Whisky.

**Smaller stemmed glass:** usually described as a Sherry glass, for Sherry, Brandy, Port and Dry Martinis.

**High ball:** (16), straight-sided and tall for long drinks, lager, beer.

1  2  3  4  5  6  7  8

# MORE GLASSES

On the other hand, if you and your family are reliable washers-up, and there is plenty of shelf space, then you may like to add more glasses to your collection. These are some to consider: Another set of slightly larger, stemmed wine glasses; these are for red wine. One usually drinks less white wine at a meal, and two elegant glasses (12, 14) standing together at each place look handsome and promising.

**Goblet:** (5) (12 oz., with or without a short stem): for water, lager and beer.
**Anjou wine glass:** long stem and more square-profiled bowl.
**Hock glass:** (7) with long stem (sometimes green or brown), for German and Alsace wines. The bowls may be lightly cut or engraved so that you can see the beautiful cool, cool colour of the wine, but please—never coloured!
**Small brandy glass:** for liqueurs and Brandy.
**Large brandy glass:** (13) balloon-shaped, for gracious or flamboyant living.
**Copita:** (6) for Sherry—very professional.
**Port glass:** (8) short stem and straighter sides.
**Cocktail glass:** (2) in all shapes, preferably not coloured. Martinis look well in a short, wide trumpet on a slim stem.
**Champagne glass:** (1, 9) the saucer-shaped Champagne glass known to all wedding guests is on the way out, and the sort with a hollow stem to show off the bubbles is rare. The current fashion is the tulip glass with a longish stem. This shares an irritating drawback with the balloon Brandy glass in that long noses (like your author's) rest on the rim opposite to the mouth, inhibiting a good angle of tilt and demanding a neck-breaking toss of the head in order to swallow from either rim.
**Liqueur glasses:** (11) any glass with a smallish bowl will do, from very modern solid glass tubes, to flights of old-fashioned fantasy, with air-twist stems, engraving—the lot. But, once again, keep in mind the gem-like colours of liqueurs, and aim for an uncoloured bowl.

10    11    12    13    14    15    16

## BASIC BAR EQUIPMENT

What, you may reasonably ask, do I need, apart from a corkscrew and a thirst? Not much, of course, but making do with a blunt knife to cut lemon peel is slow and dangerous, and stirring warm punch with a teaspoon becomes a bore if you plan to share some of these good things in your life with your friends.

1. First and most necessary is a refrigerator in which the ice compartment has a plastic ice tray, so that you can take out as many cubes as you want without difficulty.
2. A sharp knife with a serrated edge—get the cutting-up finished before the party, for obvious reasons.
3. A big jug with a measuring scale up the side, and the sort of lip with a guard to prevent the ice and so on from slipping out.
4. A long spoon for stirring.
5. A lemon squeezer is essential, and so are—
6. A strainer, and
7. A corkscrew: the wind-up or butterfly types are best.
8. Something large to put ice cubes in. The double-sided plastic containers used in bars would be fine.
9. Bottle opener.
10. A hammer and some muslin. Mint Julep, for example, requires well-crushed ice, so wrap the latter in the muslin and then duly crush it on something very solid—like the doorstep. The muslin will also be indispensable for straining the last quarter of a bottle of vintage Port.

Equipment should be kept to the essential minimum. Shops are full of tempting gadgets, but they won't improve on the functions which you can deal with if you have the things in the list above. Buy carefully and buy the best.

Note: For suggestions on glasses, see page 62.

### SOLID MEASURES

**28·352 grams = 1 ounce, but for convenience we have rounded it up to 30 grams**

15 grams = $\frac{1}{2}$ ounce
30 grams = 1 ounce
60 grams = 2 ounces
75 grams = $2\frac{1}{2}$ ounces
100 grams = $3\frac{1}{2}$ ounces
500 grams = 1 pound, $1\frac{1}{2}$ ounces
1 kilogram, 1,000 grams = 2 pounds, 3 ounces

### LIQUID MEASURES

| Metric | British | American |
|---|---|---|
| 1 litre = 1000 millilitres | = $1\frac{3}{4}$ pints | = $4\frac{1}{2}$ cups |
| 1 demilitre = 500 millilitres | = $\frac{3}{4}$ pint (generous | = 2 cups |
| 1 decilitre = 100 millilitres | = 4 fluid ounces | = $\frac{1}{2}$ cup |
| 15 millilitres | = $\frac{1}{2}$ fluid ounce | = 1 tablespoon |
| 5 millilitres | = 1 teaspoon | = 1 teaspoon |

British Imperial pint = 20 fluid ounces
American pint = 16 fluid ounces
1 British cup = $\frac{1}{2}$ pint = 10 fluid ounces
1 American cup = $\frac{1}{2}$ pint = 8 fluid ounces

## FRUIT JUICE SPECIALS

### Home-made Lemonade

Nice to serve this from a tall glass jug, with a float of lemon, lime, cucumber slices, or a sprig of mint. This recipe makes about 2 pints. Wash 3 lemons, cut them in halves and squeeze the juice. Pare off the rind very thinly and put it with 4-6 oz. of castor sugar into a basin. Add $1\frac{1}{2}$ pints of boiling water, cover, and leave until cold, stirring occasionally. Strain the liquid into a jug, add the lemon juice, and chill well before serving.

### Orangeade

This is made by the same method as the lemonade, but in the proportions of 2 oranges and 1 lemon, 2 oz. of castor sugar and 1 pint of boiling water.

### Spice Island Punch

For 10-15 glasses (about 5 pints), mix together $1\frac{1}{2}$ pints of fresh orange juice, $\frac{1}{2}$ pint of canned pineapple juice, the juice and pared rind of 1 lemon, $\frac{1}{2}$ level teaspoon each of grated nutmeg and mixed spice and 6 cloves in a big jug. Strain, chill well, and add 2 pints of ginger ale, putting crushed ice into individual glasses just before serving.

### Strawberry Crush

A year-round favourite for sweet-tooths. For about 5 servings, in stemmed goblets, put $\frac{3}{4}$ lb. of washed and hulled strawberries with $\frac{1}{2}$ pint of orange juice and sugar syrup to taste, into an electric blender to make a purée. Without a blender, just sieve the strawberries, then mix them with the orange juice and the sugar syrup. Mix equal parts of the strawberry crush with crushed ice in goblets (or tumblers) and serve at once. Suck through straws or use long spoons. A variation: If fresh limes are available, substitute them for the orange. Or use sieved raspberries instead of straw-berries.

### Somerset Cup

Take a bottle (approximately 20 oz.) of pure apple juice. Add 2 'splits' of ginger ale (about $11\frac{1}{2}$ fl. oz.), 1 can of orange juice (19 fl. oz.), $\frac{1}{2}$ pint of fresh lemon juice, a can of crushed pineapple (about 15 oz.), and stir together in a large bowl. Chill, then serve with fresh, unskinned apple wedges floating in the bowl. Add ice cubes—pretty or plain. This makes about $4\frac{1}{2}$ pints, or 9 $\frac{1}{2}$-pint mugs—the glass ones with handles.